# SPICE GIRLS
## SONG BY SONG

# SPICE GIRLS
## SONG BY SONG

### ANNE HARRISON

FONTHILL

First published in Great Britain in 2025 by
Fonthill
An imprint of
Pen & Sword Books Ltd
Yorkshire – Philadelphia

Copyright © Anne Harrison 2025

ISBN 978-1-78155-957-4

The right of Anne Harrison to be identified as Author of this work has been asserted by him in accordance with the Copyright, Designs and Patents Act 1988.

A CIP catalogue record for this book
is available from the British Library.

All rights reserved. No part of this book may be reproduced, transmitted, downloaded, decompiled or reverse engineered in any form or by any means, electronic or mechanical including photocopying, recording or by any information storage and retrieval system, without permission from the Publisher in writing. NO AI TRAINING: Without in any way limiting the Author's and Publisher's exclusive rights under copyright, any use of this publication to 'train' generative artificial intelligence (AI) technologies to generate text is expressly prohibited. The Author and Publisher reserve all rights to license uses of this work for generative AI training and development of machine learning language models.

Typeset in Sabon LT Std 10.5/13
Printed and bound in the UK by CPI Group (UK) Ltd, Croydon, CR0 4YY

The Publisher's authorised representative in the EU for product safety is Authorised Rep Compliance Ltd., Ground Floor, 71 Lower Baggot Street, Dublin D02 P593, Ireland.
www.arccompliance.com

For a complete list of Pen & Sword titles please contact

**PEN & SWORD BOOKS LIMITED**
47 Church Street, Barnsley, South Yorkshire, S70 2AS, England
E-mail: enquiries@pen-and-sword.co.uk
Website: www.pen-and-sword.co.uk

Or

PEN AND SWORD BOOKS
1950 Lawrence Rd, Havertown, PA 19083, USA
E-mail: Uspen-and-sword@casematepublishers.com
Website: www.penandswordbooks.com

*For Audrey & Joyce.
Thank you for showing a girl how it's done.*

# Preface

The Spice Girls' debut single 'Wannabe' was released on my fourth birthday and with it my brain chemistry was fundamentally altered. From the moment five girls tumbled into frame in the music video, laughing and clinging to one another on the streets of London, I was hooked. They left a trail of disorder in their wake as they tore into the Midland Grand Hotel like a tornado and then with a single word Mel B kickstarted a pop masterpiece: 'Yo!' With wide eyes, I inched closer to my family's CRT television, drinking in every detail—Geri's sequined leotard, Victoria's chic bob that I insisted resembled my own page boy haircut (readers, that was a delusional lie). By the time Mel C was doing backflips on a table, I needed a metaphorical smoke break due to sensory overload.

The obsession was immediate. They ushered me from the antiseptic world of children's entertainment into the rich realm of pop culture. Imagine going from 'The Wheels on the Bus' to 'Say You'll Be There!' What a steep jump in quality! I couldn't care less about the bus. I ride the bus every goddamn day, you can no longer interest me with your talk of buses and what their wheels may or may not do. What I *don't* get to see every day is fabulous women wearing PVC catsuits fire ray guns in the desert while a synth wails over top. It was a revelation. From that moment on, they were mine. They were the biggest pop act in the world but it didn't matter, it felt like what they were doing was for me and me alone.

Although I couldn't articulate it at the time, I think there was something liberating about watching unedited women unleashed into the world. They were far from refined and in interviews they did not sit quietly or give poised and practiced answers. In fact, they were often downright messy. They frequently all spoke over one another, abruptly veered off topic at the slightest distraction, and weren't afraid to throw questions back at interviewers and watch them sweat. For school-aged children who spent their days adhering to rules set by teachers and parents alike we were all able to live vicariously through the unfiltered behaviour of the Spice Girls. They unapologetically took up as much space as they pleased and showed what was possible when you didn't shrink your presence to please others.

As an adult, when I was feeling particularly overwhelmed by the negativity of the internet (and by extension, the world), I again turned to them for a dose of pure delight. I started looking back at the collectible photos that I'd carefully slid into the plastic sleeves of my Spice Girls photo album many years earlier. It was a nostalgia-fuelled dopamine rush but through adult eyes I was able to understand why it seemed like the Spice Girls were everywhere in the late '90s—they were. As Spicemania reached a fever pitch, the band was working at an absurd pace. Their schedule became a puzzle for me. Could I figure out where and when individual pictures were taken? For a group that would start a day in Denmark and end it in Italy, this was no easy feat. And from that a digital archive, Spice Girls Nostalgia, was born for no purpose other than to inject some positivity into my bleak online feed.

The best part about publicly sharing my love of the Spice Girls is that I never lose sight of their impact. My inbox is always teeming with messages that remind me of their enduring legacy. I hear from mothers who are thrilled to find that their young kids adore the same Girl Power anthems they did at that age. I hear from LGBTQIA+ folks for whom the Spice Girls were a buoyant lifeline, preaching self-acceptance when the messaging from all other directions was to suppress anything that went against the grain. It feels so special to share a bond with complete strangers because we have a common debt of gratitude to five women who filled our lives with music and colour and dancing and laughter and fun. We might not know each other, but I know part of your story because I understand how those exceptional flashes of joy felt. And when '2 Become 1' plays on the radio or we catch a glimpse of something seemingly insignificant, like a Spice Girls branded pencil case, we are brought right back to 1996. Youth is fleeting and so many kids, especially young girls, are forced to grow up in a hurry, so I think it's incredibly meaningful that after all these years the Spice Girls help unlock a small reserve of girlhood. Whether we're attending a rowdy screening of *Spice World The Movie* or flipping through our old Spice Girls sticker books, we are transported back to a time when our biggest problem was deciding which Spice Girl was our favourite.

The Spice Girls have been with me through it all. They make constant cameo appearances in my family photo albums, captured in snapshots of me cross-legged on the floor on Christmas morning at age six with my partially unwrapped Scary Spice doll lifted above my head triumphantly, a crazed smile plastered on my face. At recess, my friends and I laboriously rehearsed our talent show lip sync performance of 'Who Do You Think You Are' (I was Posh and while my dance moves improved slightly by showtime, my pageboy haircut absolutely did not). In high school, I worked part-time as a banquet server and the Spice Girls played at every function without fail. During every prom, every holiday party, as soon as one of their songs started my coworkers and I hurriedly tucked ourselves just out of view from guests so we could have our own little dance party. None of us ever missed a lyric. Years later when I got married, 'Wannabe' was the very first song that played at my wedding reception. The memory of all my favourite people in the world rushing to join me on the dance floor is one that I'll never forget. I hope the Spice Girls stick around for all of life's big milestones—someone be sure to play 'Saturday Night Divas' when I'm rolled into the grave. Let's go out with a bang.

Writing this book was a joy and I hope you can feel that when reading it. The Spice Girls have an incredible story and I hope your appreciation for the band deepens as you learn the history behind their iconic songs that remain as infectious and fun today as the day they were first released. In 1999, writer-producer and Spice Girls collaborator Jimmy Jam made a keen observation about what set them apart from other girl bands. 'They made you want to sing along with them,' he articulated to author David Sinclair. 'Not listen to them sing, but sing along with them.' And he was right. The music was catchy, they were entertaining in interviews, and they were stylish on red carpets, but what mattered most was that they extended the invitation to everyone. All were welcome to join them, to become a Spice Girl. So, let's press play and celebrate the people's popstars.

# Acknowledgements

Thank you to Jay Slater at Fonthill Media for reaching out with this amazing opportunity, writing this was beyond fun. Thank you to Achsah, MC, Leila, Cynthia, Monika and Natasha for holding down the fort. Kayla, for trading legal services for Thai food. Fern, for anticipatory bookmarks. Laura and Melanie, for being my early dance partners. Cara, for some sanity. Corinne, a true Spice ambassador who inspires and leads by example. Crown & Press, for letting me occupy your back corner—I should have been paying you rent. Scott & Scott, for showing me what an encyclopaedic compendium should look like. Charley, who is showing what Girl Power really means. And to the lovely people around me who kept me charged with their constant enthusiasm and encouragement: Jessica, Emilie, Marissa, Alyssa, Achsah (yes, a second shoutout), Anthony, Ashley, Kelsey, Krystine, and Meghann.

The quotes and information in this book were compiled from countless sources, please see the bibliography—I would urge any Spice fanatic to read the individual memoirs of the Spice Girls, they are fascinating accounts of what it was like to be the world's biggest popstars. Thank you to David Sinclair for writing 2004's *Wannabe*, I've read *a lot* of books about the Spice Girls but you created a wonderfully thorough telling of their story. It helped immensely when building a timeline. Thank you to Spice Girls Net for meticulously chronicling the band's career. Thank you to the readers—thank you thank you thank you! I hope this is a fun read for you.

Thanks to Mel B, Mel C, Emma, Geri, Victoria, Matt, Biff, Eliot, Andy, Paul, Rodney, LaShawn, Fred, Jimmy, and Terry for creating music that became a part of me. Thank you to the artists that kept me company over the past year as I squirreled myself away to write: primarily Sparks, Sufjan Stevens, Vampire Weekend, PUP, Bad Friends With Black Cats, Pixies, Arctic Monkeys, The Killers, My Chemical Romance, Cocteau Twins, Lana Del Rey, Talking Heads, and St Vincent. Music is the most reliably delightful part of life. Finding a new song or artist and wondering how you ever survived without them... no better feeling.

Thank you to my family! To my parents David & Monique for the encouragement and for instilling in me a love of music. Thank you for letting me skip school as a teenager to go to concerts—you were so real for that. To Paul & Melissa for being equal parts creative and kind. To Jill for being the coolest always. Kibby—I really wish I'd gotten to show you the finished product after your many check-ins. Thank you for pretending to care about the Spice Girls and for a million other things. To my Douglas and Alice who stayed glued to me for 100 per cent of the writing process. And finally, Zach. The best that's ever been. There aren't enough words. You're just a really great person and I'm so lucky that I get to be around you all the time. Sweet setup.

# Contents

| | | |
|---|---|---|
| *Preface* | | 6 |
| *Acknowledgements* | | 9 |
| *Introduction* | | 13 |
| 1 | *Spice* | 16 |
| 2 | Non-Album Tracks 1996–1997 | 56 |
| 3 | *Spiceworld* | 63 |
| 4 | Non-Album Tracks 1997–1998 | 100 |
| 5 | *Goodbye* | 105 |
| 6 | Non-Album Tracks 1999 | 113 |
| 7 | *Forever* | 117 |
| 8 | *Greatest Hits* | 140 |
| 9 | Unreleased Tracks | 145 |
| *Bibliography* | | 151 |

The casting call that started everything. (*The Stage*)

# Introduction

'R.U. 18-23 WITH THE ABILITY TO SING/DANCE? R.U. STREETWISE, OUTGOING, AMBITIOUS & DEDICATED?' read a casting call printed in the theatre publication, *The Stage*. It was drafted by Heart Management Ltd, the father-son talent manager team of Chris and Bob Herbert who felt they'd identified a gap in a market over-saturated with boy bands. '[Boy bands] only catered for 50% of the audience. I thought it would be better to put together a girl band, something sexy and sassy,' Chris reasoned in *Spice Girls: The Story of the World's Greatest Girl Band*. 'Girls would aspire to be them and guys would "admire" them.' Open auditions were held on 4 March 1994 and over 400 young women turned up to a dance studio in central London with nothing more than some sheet music and a dream, hoping to earn a spot in a girl group then tentatively named Touch. The list of 400 performers would soon be whittled down to only five.

Melanie Brown was an 18-year-old mixed-race dancer with a booming laugh and a thick Yorkshire accent. As a teenager she performed in local theatres, worked as a podium dancer in Blackpool, and as a background actor on *Coronation Street*. Equal parts charismatic and beautiful, the year before joining the Spice Girls she won a local beauty contest and was awarded the title of Miss Leeds Weekly News. She had a raw, husky voice and would soon be known globally as Scary Spice for her outspoken nature and her wardrobe of bold patterns and animal prints. She had an unbridled energy, a pierced tongue, and a firm opinion. Victoria Adams was a 19-year-old who grew up comfortably in Hertfordshire where her father had a booming wholesale company. After seeing *Fame* as a kid, Victoria threw herself into local musical theatre productions, training camps, and dance classes to distract herself from an unhappy school life where she was an outcast. Although she would come to be known for her famous pout, she also had a warm smile and a dry wit that made her disarmingly charming. As Posh Spice she built herself a reputation as a sleek and sophisticated woman of taste all the while sporting little Gucci dresses. Melanie Chisholm was a 20-year-old Liverpudlian who grew up watching her mother sing at local gigs which inspired Mel C to follow the same path. She grew up with a love of sport and her natural athleticism helped her excel at everything from karate to ballet. As a teenager, she trained at a performing arts college and grew to be an exuberant and physical performer. As Sporty Spice she stayed true to her athletic roots and opted for tracksuits instead of mini dresses, her pierced nose and tattoos breaking the typical popstar mould. She was down-to-earth, chatty, and elevated the band's music with her impressive vocal ability. Geri Halliwell was a 21-year-old jack of all trades hailing from Watford whose resumé included glamour modelling, a stint as a presenter on a Turkish gameshow, and time as a nightclub performer. She missed the first round of auditions after getting a bad sunburn on a ski holiday but used her preternatural gift of the gab to talk her way onto the shortlist, skipping ahead to the final dozen contenders. Geri wasn't a skilled dancer or a trained vocalist but she made up for it with grit, determination, and an unwavering vision that would shape the band into something sensational. With a personality as fiery as her bold red hair she was christened Ginger Spice.

The fifth girl selected was 17-year-old Michelle Stephenson who won the Herberts over with her girl-next-door looks and pretty singing voice but once rehearsals began with the four other girls, it became apparent she wasn't right for the project—her work ethic was lacking and she wasn't gelling with her bandmates. Jazz singer and Touch vocal coach Pepi Lemer proposed a former pupil, 18-year-old Emma Bunton from North London, as a replacement. The blonde-haired and blue-eyed former child model had trained at a renowned drama school and nabbed small roles in *EastEnders* and *The Bill* before getting a call from Heart Management. As the youngest of the group Emma would come to be known as Baby Spice, often sporting babydoll dresses and pigtails. Her singing voice matched her disposition, and she infused the band's tracks with a softness and a sweetness. 'As soon as I met those girls, something magic happened,' Emma reflected on the *By the Light of the Moon* podcast. 'I got in Geri's little car and I looked around and they were staring at me, all four faces, and it was like a spark of energy. It just worked immediately.' The five girls moved in together, sharing a three-bedroom house in Maidenhead where they honed their performance skills. 'For the first time in my life I was with people who wanted to know me and liked me and I had something in common with,' Victoria remarked in her memoir. 'We never stopped laughing.'

Together Melanie Brown, Victoria Adams, Melanie Chisholm, Geri Halliwell, and Emma Bunton had a crackling chemistry that made them stronger than the sum of their parts. Their unstoppable drive would end up being a hindrance to Heart Management—while outsiders may have assembled the girl group, the band alone would determine what happened next. Their music tells this story.

# 1
# *Spice*

The Spice Girls' debut album, *Spice,* was released in the UK on 4 November 1996 and promptly topped the charts in 17 countries. In the UK, it spent a total of 15 weeks at No. 1, yielded four consecutive No. 1 singles, and was the third best-selling album of the entire decade. In 1997, it was nominated for a Mercury Prize for Album of the Year, making the Spice Girls the only girl group to ever receive this prestigious nod. It also found success in America where it was the best-selling album of 1997 and the all-time best-selling debut album by a British act. It was the best-selling album in the world in 1997 and was certified multi-platinum in 27 countries. To date, *Spice* has sold over 23 million copies globally and remains the best-selling album ever released by a girl group.

'Wannabe'
Duration: 2:53
Written by Spice Girls, Matt Rowe & Richard Stannard
Produced by Matt Rowe & Richard Stannard
Mixed by Mark 'Spike' Stent
Recording engineer: Adrian Bushby
Assistant: Patrick McGovern
Keyboards and programming by Matt Rowe & Richard Stannard
Released as a single 8 July 1996

By early 1995, the Spice Girls were desperate to shed the bland pop tracks that they'd been performing ad nauseam since their formation. For the last ten months the girl group had been doggedly sharpening up their vocal harmonies and choreography skills with only generic musical numbers at their disposal; developing original material that captured their distinct viewpoint was the band's top priority and they were cautiously optimistic that songwriting duo Matt Rowe and Richard 'Biff' Stannard could help them on their mission. On a grey January day, the Spice Girls gathered in London's Strongroom Studios to test the creative waters with their new acquaintances. What they couldn't have predicted is that they were about to pen one of the decade's defining songs.

As a boy, Matt Rowe learned to play piano and sing through the Chester Cathedral Choir School. At 18, he moved to London and found assistant work at a recording studio where his duties mostly consisted of making tea for busy producers but, with a foot in the door, he began developing his technical knowledge. Richard 'Biff' Stannard, on the other hand, left school early to become a dancer. He frequented London's club scene and transitioned into the music industry when he met Tony Mortimer of the boy band East 17 and served as executive producer of the group's debut album. When Matt and Biff crossed paths in a pub, they connected over one major life goal they had in common: to write a song that went to No. 1. They joined forces and a chance encounter with the Spice Girls on 7 December 1994 would put them one step closer to their goal.

Biff was visiting Nomis Studios in Shepherd's Bush for a meeting with '80s popstar Jason Donovan but as he headed for the exit, he was accosted by an exuberant young woman in the hallway. 'Who are you?' she barked in a thick Yorkshire accent. A teenage Melanie Brown interrogated Biff, jumped on his back, and complimented his bum all within a minute of meeting. She and her four bandmates were about to perform at a talent showcase and when she learned that Biff had written and produced East 17's hit song 'Steam', she literally dragged him into the performance space. He was immediately enchanted by the group's charisma and energy. 'More than anything, they just made me laugh. I couldn't believe I'd walked into this situation. You didn't care if they were in time with the dance steps,' he told author David Sinclair for his book *Wannabe: How The Spice Girls Reinvented Pop*. 'It was something more. It just made you feel happy. Like great pop records.' Biff ran back to Matt as soon as it was over. 'I just met this amazing band,' he gushed. And just a few short weeks later, the pair were sitting down to write with the Spice Girls for the first time.

'I never work to a brief,' Biff said of the fateful session in *Music Week*, 'but the one thing I did know beforehand was that I wanted to write about how [much of a] force of nature they were.' He wanted to help them craft music that measured up to their presence offstage, a weighty task given their firecracker personalities. Ahead of the band's arrival at Strongroom, Biff developed a lively melody line inspired by 'Summer Nights' from *Grease* under which Matt set a brisk drum loop with his MPC 3000 drum machine. An image of the Spice Girls strutting along to the beat swam in their heads and they shaped the tempo and piano line to fit this commanding visual. Matt and Biff thought the backing track fit the band's attitude, now they just had to wait and see if the girls felt the same way.

The atmosphere of the studio on that winter day was laid back. The Spice Girls sat sprawled across the studio's carpeted floors, each scribbling ideas into her respective notebook, until Matt and Biff played them the unfinished musical bed. It elicited an immediate reaction and the girls sprung up with a flurry of ideas. 'They made all these different bits up,' Matt told Sinclair. 'Not thinking in terms of verse, chorus, bridge or what was going to go where, just coming up with all these sections of chanting and rapping and singing which we recorded all higgledy-piggledy.' The floodgates had burst open and the girls were experiencing what Mel B would later describe as a creative frenzy. 'It had no sit-down planning. The sentiment, the meaning, the lyrics, the rhythm, just happened,' she marvelled. With the verses and chorus already in place, Mel B and Emma proposed the idea of a call-and-response bridge: 'I'll tell you what I want, what I really really want!' Mel B exclaims on the track. 'So tell me what you want, what you really really want!' Geri quips back. Mel B wrote her rap section during a productive bathroom break. The entire song was completed in under an hour.

'I think we all realised that this was something special,' Geri later remarked in her 1999 memoir, *If Only*. 'It happened so naturally that the song seemed to symbolise what we were about.' Thematically the band simply wrote about their lives at the time. The tight-knit group spent every waking moment rehearsing and strategising about how to breakthrough in a competitive industry, so their strength as a unit was top of mind. Their bond was so intense that it was hard for outsiders, including new boyfriends, to weasel their way into the gang. 'That must be tough, going out with one of you lot and the other four hate you,' Biff interjected when the topic arose in studio. The band confirmed that if someone's new boyfriend didn't click with the rest of the group, it essentially sealed his fate: this was not going to work out. The idea was refined and it became the basis of the chorus with the lyric, 'If you wannabe my lover, you gotta get with my friends'.

Aside from a charming chorus that celebrates female friendship over disposable suitors, 'Wannabe' also contains an infamous Spice-ism.

The song's bridge concludes with Mel B declaring, 'I wanna really, really, really wanna Zig-a-zig-ah!' Upon the song's release, this newly coined term inspired a lot of discourse, with fans and critics alike debating the meaning. Guesses ranged from the uninspired (it's just gibberish!) and the mundane (that it's a reference to ZigZag brand cigarette rolling papers) to the downright preposterous (conspiracies that it's coded religious messaging). In 2015, *The Sun* ran an article in which an alleged insider claimed that it bafflingly meant 'shit and cigars'. According to the anonymous source, a male pop performer was also working in Strongroom during the *Spice* sessions and the girls noticed him for all the wrong reasons. 'This guy had this nasty habit of taking a dump in the shared khazi while smoking a cigar, so we took to referring to him as Shit and Cigars. During the recording this phrase was thrown around a lot and must have worked its way into Mel B's subconscious,' said the source. The band always said it meant whatever an individual wanted it to mean but Mel C finally pulled back the curtain in her 2022 memoir, *The Sporty One*. 'I can't remember exactly how Zig-a-zig-ah came about but in the song, it means sex,' she wrote. 'I hope I've not broken some secret Spice Girl code!' For some, this answer was still too vague and the questions persisted about what sexual act this was referencing. But the Spice Girls have remained tight-lipped. 'I made up that word, and I can't tell you,' Mel B said firmly during a January 2024 appearance on *Today with Hoda & Jenna*. 'If I do, I will have to kill you, and we don't want to do that.'

Although concealed in innuendo, it's fitting that this Girl Power anthem includes references to female sexual desire. 'Wannabe' was written in the mid 1990s amid the emergence of third-wave feminism, a period in which women sought to redefine femininity and sexuality on an individual level and, by extension, shed sexual constraints. Female identity was no longer one-size-fits-all and women were empowered to explore their options. A piece by *Time* revealed that over the course of the decade the median age of marriage increased from 20 to 25, meaning that single and childfree women could pursue careers in traditionally male-dominated industries and secure greater financial independence for themselves. This also meant sexual self-actualisation was more within reach and women could determine what they wanted and, maybe more importantly, what they didn't want. What the Spice Girls wanted was apparently quite simple: they wanted to be satisfied by men who weren't jerks to their friends.

Absent from the momentous 'Wannabe' writing session was one key member of the group. The Spice Girls had spent a productive few days working on new music with Matt and Biff and decided to capitalise on the momentum and continue working through the weekend. This posed an issue for Victoria, who was under pressure to attend a family wedding of her then-boyfriend. She was unenthusiastic about attending the nuptials of people she didn't even know and was especially hesitant about missing important developments with the band. The other four girls assured her that if anything notable happened they would keep her in the loop and encouraged her to attend the wedding—Geri and Victoria had both recently purchased their first ultramodern (albeit bulky) mobile phones and they were ready to put their cutting-edge technology to use. And so, with all her bandmates nestled inside the Shoreditch studio, Victoria begrudgingly stepped away and began her trek to Torquay.

Geri kept her promise and diligently phoned Victoria with regular updates and invited her to share feedback about the direction of 'Wannabe' but from the moment she received the first call Victoria had a sinking feeling. She knew she should be in the room with the rest of the group and that giving yes or no answers down the line couldn't compare to being part of the collaborative environment in studio. Her dismay was amplified by her immediate understanding that 'Wannabe' was special. This wasn't just a song, this was *the* song. It was undeniable. This song was their group identity distilled into a pithy pop track.

Later, the other girls tried to reassure Victoria that missing the 'Wannabe' writing session wasn't a big deal, but their words of consolation fell flat. Privately, Victoria wept with regret. Aside from missing a pivotal moment in the band's history, there were also verifiable consequences for her absence. The song was structured so that every girl had her moment to shine—everyone, that is, except Victoria. While Mel B, Mel C, Emma, and Geri each had solo lines that showcased their individual personalities, Victoria was relegated to the role of backup singer. This instantly weighed on Victoria, who was certain that listeners would dismiss her as the expendable band member who didn't even sing. She expressed this fear to her mother who reassured her that no one would even notice. After all, this was just one song of many. In subsequent years, however, Victoria felt vindicated about her worries in 1995. Jokes were consistently made about Victoria's singing ability (or alleged lack thereof) and critics often reduced her contributions to posing and pouting. She attributes this misconception to the chain reaction that began when she missed the writing of 'Wannabe'.

The track underwent minimal revisions between writing and recording, with only two notable adjustments to the top of the track.

The patter of Mel B's footsteps running up to the microphone was added, as well as a brash laugh right before the song begins, a laugh that is often misattributed to Mel B. 'Well, that's Geri's cackle isn't it,' Mel C clarified during a 2020 *Gaydio* interview. 'I can't remember what was being laughed at but I'm sure it was something very rude knowing the Spice Girls,' she said with a cackle of her own. While writing and recording was an unusually smooth process, mixing was a more time-intensive affair. 'We were working 18-hour days, seven days a week,' Biff said. 'We wrote 'Wannabe' quite quickly, but it took ages to get it to sound right. I remember waking up on the studio floor with this post-it from Matt saying, "Press play". We'd finally got it.'

By this time, the Spice Girls had grown frustrated with the inexperience of Heart Management and were on a quest to find the right representation. 'Wannabe' became a critical part of the equation. 'Our calling card, if you like, was "Wannabe",' Victoria wrote in her 2001 memoir *Learning to Fly*. 'It said everything about us, musically and in terms of where we were coming from.' They established a solid routine that put the song front and centre. The five girls would arrive at an appointment with a prospective manager and burst into the meeting space with intensity, switching on their portable stereo from which the demo of 'Wannabe' would blare. Then the Spice Girls put on a show. They danced on boardroom tables, they climbed on furniture, on a few occasions they literally rolled in on roller-skates. Why just tell executives about their star power when they could show them? 'Once you'd been "spiced", you didn't forget it,' Geri said of their tactic. This daring approach helped them land Simon Fuller of 19 Entertainment as a manager in the spring of 1995. 'It was quite unusual to have these five young girls come bounding in the office with confidence and say, "You have to manage us, and we're not leaving until you agree",' Simon laughed in a 2022 *The New York Times* article. 'It was just very contagious, that energy.' On 13 July 1995, they signed a record deal with Virgin Records.

'It seemed obvious to all of us that "Wannabe" would be our first single,' Victoria recalled in her memoir. Regrettably for the band, however, not everyone agreed: both Simon and Virgin didn't think 'Wannabe' was the right choice. They felt it wasn't a smooth introduction to the band and was maybe even off-putting as a first impression to listeners. 'But just as we'd known about our name, our image, our music, everything, us five knew, without doubt, that 'Wannabe' had to be our first single,' Mel C insisted. Geri didn't mince words either. 'I thought, this is bullshit!' she railed in her memoir. '"Wannabe" is our signature tune. The more they tried to persuade me, the more certain I was that they were wrong. I felt anxious but also empowered. I knew what the other girls thought; we were agreed on this.' Fortunately, the group had negotiated a contract that ceded ultimate creative control to the Spice Girls themselves and they told Simon and the label that this was non-negotiable—the first single had to be 'Wannabe'. Virgin acquiesced but not before attempting to 'fix' the track by sending it to American producer Dave Way who reimagined it with an R&B swing sound. The girls were frustrated that it no longer sounded like a classic pop song and after voicing this to Virgin, Dave's mix was abandoned. The original mix was then lightly tweaked by engineer Mark Stent, known for his work alongside Madonna, Depeche Mode, and Pet Shop Boys, to sound less tinny and more radio ready.

When the Spice Girls started brainstorming ideas for their debut music video, they envisioned a splashy production set in a high-end Barcelona hotel but when director Johan Camitz was unable to get the necessary permits, the group had to temper their expectations and do some location scouting closer to home. On the evening of 19 April 1996, the Spice Girls descended upon the run-down Midland Grand Hotel located next-door to St. Pancras station in North London. Although the area was revitalised in subsequent years (and the hotel upgraded and renamed) it was in disrepair during the Spice Girls' shoot. The area was suffering a period of urban decay with unemployment and poverty driving crime rates up, something that the Spice Girls were conscious of as they lingered in the street, their uneasy feelings exacerbated by the darkness of the night shoot. Inside, the crew worked to transform the bare and deteriorating space into something that appeared grand on camera. Lighting was set up strategically and velvet was draped along the walls to make unsightly spaces seem luxurious.

'The central idea for the video was to recreate the same energy and dynamism that we showed when we crashed into record companies and did the frenetic hard sell,' Geri recounted in her memoir. 'We invaded places and left people breathless.' The video features the Spice Girls running rampant through the stuffy property—singing, jumping, and dancing with an alternating cast of eccentric characters as they tear through the space. (When the Spice Girls attended the 1996 BRIT Awards as unknowns a couple months earlier, an inexperienced Geri asked soon-to-be Prime Minister Tony Blair to be one of the extras. He declined.) The routine was rehearsed dozens of times on that unseasonably cold April night prior to filming because it was fast-paced and required coordination with numerous extras. At one point Mel C had to do a backflip on a banquet table adorned with candelabras, flower arrangements and table settings, something pulled directly from one of their real-life cold calls, but an ambitious component to achieve in step with all the other aspects of the video. 'That was quite challenging,' Mel C recalled. 'And when I say challenging, I mean terrifying. I did it, though. All those years of gymnastics didn't half pay off.' Geri was determined to look tall and modelesque and wore a towering pair of vintage Mary Quant platform shoes to achieve this. She struggled to even walk in the pumps so running through the halls on cue was nearly impossible. She fell repeatedly, sometimes narrowly avoiding taking lamps, or other people, down with her. At one point she almost careened down a flight of stairs. It took countless takes to create a video that appeared to be one continuous shot. In reality, the finished product was two takes seamlessly stitched together with footage captured by a single camera operator who chased the girls around the hotel with a Steadicam strapped to his torso until they wrapped in the early hours of the morning.

Even in this first music video, the Spice Girls' individual senses of style are already well-defined. The group was allotted a small wardrobe budget for the shoot but almost all of it went towards Mel B's cropped lime green Calvin Klein tank and a stylish pair of Jean Paul Gaultier trousers. Ironically, it was this premium ensemble that later caused an issue—Mel B's tight top in combination with that night's frigid conditions resulted in her erect nipples being visible beneath the fabric, a detail that later led to the video being banned in certain parts of Asia. The other four girls donned outfits that caused far less controversy: Geri wore a sequined showgirl leotard that she picked up from a second-hand stall at Notting Hill Market for only £20; Mel C wore Adidas tracksuit bottoms and a halter top; Emma wore a virginal white minidress; and Victoria, of course, was in a little black dress (although at this time it was an inexpensive dress from Miss Selfridge, and not Gucci). These looks were distinct and memorable and would inspire decades of Halloween costumes to come.

Virgin was unimpressed with the footage from the 'Wannabe' video shoot and immediately deemed it unsuitable for commercial release. Simon Fuller was tasked with delivering the bad news to the Spice Girls and he did his best to explain why the video wasn't up to par and would need to be reshot: it wasn't polished enough to compete with music videos in America, the girls were visibly wobbly on their feet as they sprinted around the set, it was too chaotic, the lighting was too dark, the footage was shoddy and, of course, there were objections to Mel B's visible nipples. Overall, there weren't many positives. But the band was happy with the finished product. 'It perfectly captured what had happened over the last year or two; us barging our way into the music industry and causing a right mess,' Mel C stated in her autobiography. 'Shoot it again? I don't think so.' Geri thought that the details Virgin was complaining about were features, not bugs. 'It wasn't very controlled—we didn't want it to be. We wanted the camera to capture the madness of Spice,' she explained. An additional stressor on the girls was the video's financing. It cost £130,000 to produce and the expense was split 50/50 between the record label and the future earnings of the Spice Girls. This was a lean time for the group and it seemed ridiculous to scrap a video they adored, wasting thousands of pounds in the process. Yet again, the five girls banded together to defend their vision and overrule the label. Under pressure, Virgin decided to do a trial run of 'Wannabe' on *The Box*, a cable channel that broadcast music videos across the UK and Ireland, and following the video's first airing, the station was bombarded with replay requests. At the same time, DJs began incorporating the song into club mixes. This traction bolstered the Spice Girls' claim that 'Wannabe' could be an impactful debut single. With this data in hand, the team prepared for the song's formal release.

'Wannabe' was released in the United Kingdom on 8 July 1996 and a week later, the Spice Girls gathered at Geri's stepsister's home to listen to Capital FM's Top 40 countdown with Dr Fox, anxiously waiting to hear how their single had performed. The girls sat on a picnic blanket, the sun blazing above them, waiting breathlessly for 'Wannabe' to be mentioned as the numbers steadily decreased. Upon learning that 'Wannabe' had debuted at No. 3, they erupted into celebration. 'We hugged and danced around the garden in bare feet,' Geri recounted in her memoir. '[My stepsister] took a picture of us all sitting on the picnic rug holding up three fingers. Later, I had it framed because it showed such a wonderful moment in our lives.' On 20 July 1996, the Spice Girls were having dinner at their hotel in Tokyo during a promotional visit to Japan when their personal assistant rushed over to their table. 'Simon has a message for you all,' she beamed. 'He says you should crack open a bottle of bubbly because 'Wannabe' is No. 1.' The Spice Girls had topped the UK charts with their very first single, with a song everyone else had discounted, a song the five girls had to defend every step of the way.

In a favourable review for *Vox*, Stephen Dalton wrote that, 'the terrific "Wannabe" kicks proceedings off with its cartoonish war-cry opening, lusty pop-rap beat and high-speed torrent of saucy innuendo'. Paul Gorman for *Music Week* praised the song for being 'smart, witty, abrasive and downright fun'. While 'Wannabe' undeniably won the band many fans and kickstarted Spicemania, critical reception of the track was mixed, a trend that would persist throughout the band's career. Dan Cairns of *The Sunday Times* posited that the Spice Girls were assembled just to sell 'crop tops and other minimal garments to young girls'. He did, however, go on to reluctantly admit that 'Wannabe' was, '2 minutes and 53 seconds of pop perfection'. Christina Kelly for *Rolling Stone* described the song as 'a watered-down mix of hip-hop and cheesy pop balladry'. Whether positive or negative, one thing was for sure: everyone was talking about the Spice Girls.

'Wannabe' held on to the top spot on the UK charts for seven consecutive weeks and by the end of 1996 the song had reached No. 1 in 22 countries; this figure would eventually rise to 37 as the group's popularity continued to swell in international markets. In January 1997, the single was released in the United States where it beat a 32-year record held by The Beatles with 'I Want to Hold Your Hand' when it achieved the highest chart entry by a British group's debut. In 1997, the song was awarded both the prestigious Ivor Novello Award for Best-Written British Single and the BRIT Award for British Single of the Year. It remains the worldwide all-time best-selling single by an all-female group with over 2 million chart sales. The quintet also successfully endured the shift from physical media to streaming—2020 Spotify statistics revealed that 'Wannabe' was the most-streamed '90s song by a female artist and on 31 December 2023, it surpassed a billion streams on the platform. In 2014, a study by Manchester's Museum of Science and Industry determined that it was the most recognisable pop song of all time after participants in a survey were able to identify it in an average of just 2.29 seconds, faster than they could identify any other hit song from the past 60 years. 'As much as they were sitting down trying to be musos and write songs, there was a lot of jumping around and being stupid,' Biff told *Music Week* in 2007, reflecting on the convivial session from which 'Wannabe' emerged. 'I thought if you can tap into that and capture it on the record, that's when you'll create the excitement.' By imbuing 'Wannabe' with a sense of unapologetic fun, an entire generation felt compelled to join the party.

## 'Say You'll Be There'
Duration: 3:55
Written by Spice Girls & Eliot Kennedy
Additional writing credit to Jon B.
Produced by Absolute

Mixed by Mark 'Spike' Stent
Recording engineer: Jeremy Wheatley
Assistant: Adam Brown
All instruments by Absolute except harmonica by Judd Lander
Released as a single 14 October 1996

After the release of 'Wannabe' many critics assumed that the Spice Girls would fade into obscurity, doomed to be a one hit-wonder in the footnotes of pop history. A September 1996 edition of *Music Week* asserted that the band's next single would be the true test of their long-term potential and so the girl group sprang into action planning their follow-up. 'Say You'll Be There' was a bold and empowered track that ordered partners to walk the talk, all the while weaving a throughline of female unity and, above all, it was an intensely catchy pop blitz. Despite public scepticism, pre-sale numbers for 'Say You'll Be There' were the highest ever recorded by Virgin. 'Say You'll Be There' was released on 14 October 1996, and, with 350,000 copies sold in the first week, it went straight to No. 1 in the UK as early metrics predicted. Internationally, it climbed to Top 10 positions in over a dozen countries. While 'Wannabe' put the Spice Girls on the map, 'Say You'll Be There' proved that their success was not a fluke—yet unthinkably this career-defining song almost didn't materialize when the Spice Girls' opportunity to work with co-writer Eliot Kennedy nearly slipped away.

After casting a new girl group in March 1994, the team at Heart Management, fronted by Chris Herbert and his father Bob, decided to deliberately withhold contracts from the Spice Girls. They wanted the girls to feel like the group lineup was still fluid and any one of them could be replaced without a second thought. This, the Herberts reasoned, would keep the girls desperate to prove themselves and would afford Heart more control. While this tactic to keep the band in line may have initially been effective, the power shifted as friendships within the group deepened and their collective chemistry was validated by writers and producers in the industry. The girls were now aware that they had options. By the time Heart presented them with contracts in February 1995, the Spice Girls had soured on the father-son team. '[For them] suddenly it was, "Shit, we didn't get them to sign". Whereas for us it was, "Shit, thank goodness we didn't sign",' Victoria wrote of the sudden role reversal. 'Although I didn't know much about contracts, this one seemed to be very much in their favour,' Geri recalled. 'Effectively, we'd be owned by the management team and have no say in the music, marketing or promotion of Spice.' When Heart applied pressure to sign, the girls instead packed up their stuff and fled the house they shared in Maidenhead, leaving a note on the kitchen table. 'Thank you for all you have done. We can't agree to the terms of your contract.'

The Spice Girls were exhilarated to be free of management that wouldn't afford them creative license but within this elation a new fear surfaced. Heart Management had scheduled a writing session for the Spice Girls with record producer Eliot Kennedy and without his contact information they worried that they'd squandered their chance to work with him. Eliot was a Sheffield-based producer and songwriter who began writing music with his brother at age 13 before beginning an apprenticeship at a local recording studio where he learned how to operate recording equipment. As a young adult he was involved in a car accident and he used the resulting insurance payment to buy his own recording equipment. He stayed in his hometown of Sheffield and built a solid reputation in the area as a freelance engineer. He produced Lulu's 'Independence', Dannii Minogue's 'This Is The Way', and Kenny Thomas' 'Destiny' before collaborating with Take That. Eliot's impressive body of work made the Spice Girls desperate to work with him.

'So, off we went to Sheffield,' Mel B recollected in her 2002 memoir *Catch A Fire*. She and Geri planned to scour an entire city for their prospective songwriting partner. '[We were] thinking we're going to find this writer; we're going to find him and we're going to explain our situation and see if he will still work with us. We can't pay him because we can't afford it but we're going to see if this will work.' The duo hit the road in Geri's ailing Fiat Uno and pulled into a service station to consult a local phone book. 'We phoned three numbers, and the third number was [his studio],' Mel B remarked. An employee gave them Eliot's address and with that the pair hit the road, pulling into Eliot's driveway after midnight.

Eliot was shocked to find Mel B and Geri on the other side of his door. 'They just drove to Sheffield, which is 160 miles north of where they were in London, and descended on my doorstep,' Eliot said. The girls pleaded their case to Eliot who responded with kindness and opened his door to the burgeoning popstars. Mel C, Victoria, and Emma joined soon after. 'So, literally I adopted five sisters, which anyone with sisters will know is not an easy thing to do,' Eliot laughed during a 2023 interview with the *Richmond Sentinel*. 'But they were incredible. Their energy was amazing. It was like having five hurricanes move into your house, but it was also so inspiring.' The Spice Girls were inspired by this important step forward as well. 'Out of the whole of Sheffield, we managed to track down this guy and it was just like... this is it, there's no stopping us now, we can do what we want,' Mel B recalled emotionally.

The Spice Girls turned to songwriting as a distraction from the turmoil of their management shakeup. 'None of them played instruments, so I was left to do the music and get that vibe together,' said Eliot. He played some chords on the piano, the first fragments of what would become 'Say You'll Be There'. 'What I said to them was, "Look, I've got a chorus - check this out". Then they were throwing lines at us. Ten minutes later the song was written,' Eliot remarked. '[I]t was a real quick process. They were confident in what they were doing.' The song was the first track ever recorded in Eliot's new home studio and he christened the space 'Spice' in honour of the occasion. 'We recorded it in our trakkies and socks,' Mel C said. 'It was a cool vibe—dead laid-back.' An alternate version of the track that included a Mel B rap section was written however this was omitted from the final cut. The recorded demo was passed along to Paul Wilson and Andy Watkins at Absolute who produced the track to have a soulful undercurrent. The final version of the song opens with a distorted piano line, as though being played on an old turntable, before a hasty electronic kick launches the listener forward into a megawatt hook. The song delivers synthesizer runs, solo sections for each of the five girls, and a musical interlude with a harmonica solo courtesy of Judd Lander of 'Karma Chameleon' fame, all of which are tied together by an ear-worm chorus. 'I'm giving you everything / All that joy can bring, this I swear / And all that I want from you / Is a promise you will be there.' American singer-songwriter Jon B would be credited on later versions of the track because the melody line of his 1995 song 'What U R 2 Me' for American R&B group After 7 bore a resemblance to the chorus of 'Say You'll Be There'. In 2021, a 25th anniversary edition of *Spice* was released including a 'Say You'll Be There' 7' Radio Mix, a slower arrangement that replaced Judd Lander's harmonica with a groovy saxophone solo.

On 7 September 1996, the Spice Girls trekked out to California's Mojave Desert to start their two-day video shoot for the 'Say You'll Be There' music video. Both visually and conceptually, the video was a dramatic departure from 'Wannabe'. While their first video was a slice-of-life romp, 'Say You'll Be There' was a conceptual and visual statement. It drew inspiration from the 1965 exploitation film *Faster, Pussycat! Kill! Kill!* by writer-director Russ Meyer in which three go-go dancers embark on a murder spree in the California desert. The Spice Girls ditched their signature styles in exchange for sleek PVC ensembles that straddled the line between intimidating and chic, transforming the quintet into fantastical alter-egos in a nod to the B-movie source material. Like the opening sequence of a film, the video opens with an introductory character montage, complete with title cards introducing viewers to the feature's protagonists: Geri was Trixie Firecracker, Victoria was Midnight Miss Suki, Mel C was Katrina Highkick, Emma was Kung Fu Candy, and Mel B was Blazin' Bad Zula. The Spice Girls tear across the desert in a Petty Blue Dodge Charger Daytona with a kidnapped mystery man bound to the roof of their car in a symbolic overpowering of male dominance. These cinematic tableaus are intercut with performances from the Spice Girls in front of a glittering mirrored backdrop, a dazzling contrast to the dull desert terrain stretching out behind them. Ahead of the shoot, a martial arts instructor had shown the girls some moves and on the day Emma, the daughter of a Gojukai Karate club operator and blue belt holder herself, gave her bandmates pointers on proper combative posture. The Spice Girls fire ray guns and throw lethal boomerangs on their rampage.

The sleek and sexy costumes were a source of anxiety for the video's director, Vaughan Arnell, who feared that they would be too hot for TV. When he arrived on set and saw the wardrobe pieces that the stylist had assembled, he began panicking. 'I couldn't believe it,' he remarked in a 2016 *Mirror* interview. 'I almost died! I was seriously wetting myself, let me tell you. I just thought, "How the hell are we going to put them in this?" It was all Spandex and leather and it was just pure sex shop.' He bit his tongue and proceeded according to plan, secretly thinking the video may never see the light of day.

Racy or not, the wardrobe presented another issue during filming—the already overwhelming heat of the desert was exacerbated by all the black material and the girls felt like they were being cooked alive. While both days of the shoot had early start times to escape the brunt of the midday sun, it helped very little and by the time hair and makeup was complete, the sun was already at full force. Geri and Victoria fared the worst as their wardrobes were the most burdensome. Geri wore skin-tight PVC shorts and a matching midriff-baring top with fire-red thigh-high leather boots. 'My makeup melted like ice cream and the frames of my sunglasses were too hot to touch,' Geri shared. Victoria had it worst of all with a full-body form-fitting PVC catsuit. 'Poor Victoria […] the director had her balancing on the back of a car for more than an hour,' Geri wrote in her memoir. 'She nearly fainted in the heat just for three seconds of footage.' Vaughan was impressed with how she handled the difficult working conditions and, unbeknownst to Victoria at the time, she was also impressing her future-husband. '[David Beckham later] told me that he'd seen me in Russia,' Victoria revealed in her autobiography. 'It was an England game and he was sharing a room with Gary Neville and they were watching MTV when the 'Say You'll Be There' video came on. David had said to Gary, I really like the one in the black catsuit, the one with the bob.'

After an exhausting day in the sun, the Spice Girls retreated to a small hotel on the outskirts of the desert. They turned the air conditioning up full blast, rehydrated, and got some rest, knowing that they would soon be back out in the blistering heat for the second and final day of the shoot. When the others retreated to bed early, Mel B and Geri borrowed a car and set off back into the desert. They parked in the middle of nowhere and admired the night sky from the roof. 'I'd never seen so many stars,' Geri reminisced. 'I felt as if the roof of the universe had come down to touch my nose.' Mel B was also in awe of the view. 'All around us was pitch black; the car was the only source of light for miles and miles.' On a whim they decided to tear off their clothes and streak into the unending dark of the desert. 'It was such a laugh, a very special moment, an ecstatic, giddy buzz like no other,' Mel B recalled fondly in her memoir. Although the experience of making 'Say You'll Be There' gifted the girls with lasting memories, not all of them were positive. Two weeks after filming wrapped the band got a sneak peek at the footage and they quickly noticed that one girl was featured more heavily than the other four. 'We'd always set out to do everything totally equally; no lead singer, no spokesperson, everything split five ways, no one was more important than the other,' Mel C later reflected. 'A fight broke out, voices were raised, and in a huge huff, Geri decided she was leaving the band.' Tensions were diffused, the edit was fixed, and Geri ultimately stayed but the ordeal foreshadowed future vulnerabilities.

Critical reception at the time was mixed despite the single's clear commercial success. The Spice Girls were supremely polarising and were either embraced by critics as a breath of fresh air or seen as a harbinger of death for the music industry. While some lambasted the song for being superficial drivel from a manufactured act, others applauded the track as a home run and set aside preconceived notions about the band's origins with Dele Fadele of *NME* describing the 'monstrously catchy tune' as state-of-the-art pop music. 'Say You'll Be There' won both the 1996 Smash Hits Award for Best Pop Video and the 1997 BRIT Award for British Video of the Year.

## '2 Become 1'

Duration: 4:01
Written by Spice Girls, Matt Rowe & Richard Stannard
Produced by Matt Rowe & Richard Stannard
Additional production and mix by Andy Bradfield
Recording engineer: Adrian Bushby
Assistant: Patrick McGovern
Keyboards and programming by Matt Rowe & Richard Stannard
Additional programming by Paul Waller, Pete Davis & Statik
Guitar by Greg Lester
Strings arranged by Craig Armstrong
Orchestral contractor: Isobel Griffiths Ltd
Orchestral leader: Perry Montague-Mason
Released as a single 16 December 1996

The Spice Girls wrote '2 Become 1' with Biff Stannard and Matt Rowe in early 1995 shortly after completing 'Wannabe' together. The shift from writing high-octane pop pieces to tender ballads was an organic progression in the studio where things were getting flirtatious between Geri and Matt. The budding romance was an open secret amongst their fellow collaborators and Mel B noticed the palpable chemistry between the pair. 'When Matt and Geri started making eyes at each other, I knew what was going on, even though they denied it, I knew them both too well for it to be a secret from me,' she remarked in her memoir. Biff made similar observations. 'I don't want to get into that side of things. They were close,' Biff relented, clearly uncomfortable divulging any personal details about his peers. 'They clicked. And I think the lyrics in '2 Become 1' came from that, especially the first verse, which they wrote together.' Matt himself would admit to flirting but maintained that things always stayed professional. He did, however, elaborate on the connection they shared as a group. 'We were all very close,' Matt explained in Sinclair's *Wannabe*. 'That was the thing that I think was a big part of the music being so successful. It was done with a lot of love. We really loved them. I think they loved us as well. It wasn't really a financial exercise. It was a labour of love.'

'2 Become 1' showcased a much softer side of the Spice Girls and helped dismantle any accusations that the act was a one-trick pony. For the first time, synthesizer runs and bouncy keyboard lines were swapped for delicate acoustic guitar solos and the tempo was slowed to a sensual pulse. The song culminates with a 30 second orchestral outro arranged by composer Craig Armstrong, a sweeping and sophisticated conclusion to a ballad with lyrics full of intensity and yearning, unmatched by the band's previous songs in its striking sincerity. The track took a full week to record in December 1995 as the Spice Girls experimented with how to emote in a way that translated to their vocals. 'Now you can do two songs in a day, easily,' Mel C remarked in her 2022 memoir. 'We all had to figure out mic-controls and ad-libs and punching in. It was an intense learning period for all of us.' Geri in particular struggled. Her unpolished vocal style was perfect for punchy tracks that benefitted from a dry, personality-laden delivery but he was acutely aware of her shortcomings when a song demanded more finesse. 'Having had no vocal training, I found it difficult to relax and deliver emotion. Nervousness tends to make your voice go higher and thinner,' she remembered. Geri recorded and re-recorded her lines countless times for '2 Become 1', running take after take until 4am when she, Matt, and Biff were finally satisfied with the results. She later confessed in her memoir, *If Only*, that she was only able to deliver the appropriate level of warmth by going to a dark place mentally—her father had passed away in 1993 and thinking of how much she missed him helped her deliver her lines with conviction, tears springing to her eyes as the music swelled behind her.

With assistance from writer and translator N. Maño, the Spice Girls recorded a Spanish language version of '2 Become 1' as a bonus track for Latin American and South African versions of *Spice*. There are also multiple English versions—between the November 1996 release of their debut album and the December release of the song as a single it underwent a lyrical amendment. 'Any deal that we endeavour, boys and girls feel good together,' Geri sings in the second verse of the album version. This was replaced by Victoria crooning, 'Once again if we endeavour, love will bring us back together', after the group realised that the heteronormative original did not align with their message of inclusion. 'We changed the lyrics in a hotel,' Emma stated as reported by *NME*. 'We were travelling, and we were like, "Absolutely, it needs to be changed." We felt like it needed to be more inclusive.'

Allyship was a key part of the Spice Girls' ideology from inception. 'The Spice Girls were about embracing individuality,' Mel C emphatically told *Pink News*. 'Everybody was invited into our gang. It wasn't just Girl Power, it was Gay Power.' As a young woman in the public eye who didn't adhere to prescribed gender norms through fashion, Mel C's own sexuality was often subject to speculation from ignorant tabloids but she used these invasive attacks to advocate a message of acceptance. 'I had zero problem with people thinking I was gay,' she reflected in 2022.

'If I was gay, so what? It's not a bad thing, it's a brilliant thing.' The Spice Girls were quickly iconised by the queer community and the band credits their success to this early support. 'I think it's been everything and they've been there for us from the very, very start,' Mel B reflected. 'Without them, it wouldn't have really happened, I don't think.' A lot of the Spice Girls' larger-than-life stage garments, hairstyling and makeup were influenced by the drag community and LGBTQIA+ designers, so the band saw their relationship with the community as one built on mutual admiration. 'Quite often, young boys come up to me on the street and say, "You made it OK for me to come out and not hide anymore and really celebrate and be who I was scared to be",' Victoria shared. 'That means so much.' During the Spice Girls' 2019 reunion tour, the band sold T-shirts that proudly decreed the Spice Girls manifesto: We welcome all ages, all gender identities, all countries of origin, all sexual orientations, all religions & beliefs, all abilities. Back in 1996, when casual homophobia and prejudice was often left unchallenged, the Spice Girls wanted to ensure their music was a safe space for everyone. And that meant making '2 Become 1' a love song for all types of love.

'It's basically a love song, but it's got a message—make sure you put a condom on if you're going to have sex. We all think that's very important,' Mel B wrote in 1997's *Real Life, Real Spice: The Official Story*, highlighting another consequential lyric in '2 Become 1'. Towards the song's close Emma sweetly purrs, 'Be a little bit wiser baby / Put it on, put it on'. This safe sex messaging was a product of the times— the first reported cases of AIDS occurred in June 1981 and it shaped the world through the next two decades, claiming nearly half a million lives in the United States by the year 2000. AIDS-related deaths began to decrease in the early 1990s as scientific advancements led to the development of medications that allowed HIV-positive individuals to live normal lives with undetectable and untransmittable statuses. Yet as the pressing danger began to recede, many were left reeling from the collective trauma. The Spice Girls were not the only musical act of the decade to incorporate messages about responsible sexual practices: 'Let's Talk About Sex' by Salt-n-Pepa, 'The What' by The Notorious B.I.G., and 'Look Who's Burnin'' by Ice Cube all positively reference condom use prior to the release of '2 Become 1'. These attempts to normalise contraceptive use proposed a new reality where sex could be reclaimed as liberating, enjoyable, and safe if approached responsibly. The Spice Girls also frame the use of protection as something done out of respect for your partner, not as a hassle that hinders pleasure. For the Spice Girls' young fanbase the message may not have fully landed, but it helped set a precedent—if Baby Spice was insistent on practicing safe sex perhaps listeners could expect the same courtesy from their partners.

The Spice Girls also challenged restrictive gender norms with the language they choose to employ when discussing sex. 'We can achieve it', Mel B sings with conviction. 'Let's work it out', Mel C later implores. 'In the song, sex isn't something men do to women, nor is it a spectacle of hard work and seduction put on by girls while men sit back and enjoy the show,' wrote journalist and pop-culture commentator Lauren Bravo in her 2018 book *What Would the Spice Girls Do?* 'It's something both parties muck in and do together.' This reframing of power dynamics was subtle, but it presented a symbiotic partnership as a reasonable expectation, a healthy lesson for the band's young female fanbase to internalize. While snide reviews made quips about the band's weak voices and wardrobe choices, a whole generation was exposed to concepts like sex positivity and feminism through the Spice Girls. While their messaging may have lacked an academic level of refinement, as any pop song would, that didn't mean it was without value. During a time when *Cosmopolitan* was running their millionth article about how to please your man, the Spice Girls had a different approach. 'The one rule was that we wouldn't write a love song,' Mel B explained. 'Our mission was to tell men what we wanted from them instead.'

The music video for '2 Become 1' has a moodier visual language than the Spice Girls' previous two videos. They drift across New York City in the dark of night as the diffused lights of the city dance around them at full speed, layered up in plush, jewel-toned coats. They deliver lyrics in intimate closeups near New York City landmarks such as Radio City Music Hall, the Brooklyn Bridge, the ice rink at Rockefeller Center, and, of course, a Sbarro. 'We just had this image of an empty New York,' director Andy Delaney recalled on a 2023 episode of the *90s Noise* podcast. 'You can explore and it's your own playground.'

'It looked like we were in New York, and it was very cold and snowy, but no we weren't in America,' Emma revealed to *Heart* in 2021. 'We were actually in a studio in London somewhere.' Prior to the Spice Girls' involvement, Andy Delaney and Monty Whitebloom, a directing team known as Big TV!, travelled to the US to spend a week filming the darkened streets of New York City at a slow shutter speed, blurring any motion captured into streaks of light. While Andy and Monty originally planned to remove the streaks, leaving just empty streets, the dancing lights looked so beautiful that they decided to leave them unedited. Each second of the video required several minutes of recording time so for five nights straight the crew filmed from 6pm to 5am. The Spice Girls began their two-day shoot at a studio on Old Compton Street on 5 November 1996 and performed in front of green screens; the city backdrop was digitally inserted during post-production. '[It] was really cold because there were a load of wind machines going,' Mel C recalled. 'It was funny because we wanted to get this effect of our hair blowing really slowly in the wind, so we had to lip sync in double time. It was hilarious singing so fast.' As the girls worked with focus inside the studio, chaos raged outside. 'They were at the height of their mania and there were hundreds of kids who had somehow found out where the video was being shot—it was like Beatlemania,' Andy said. 'It was insane. You'd have to fight through crowds [to get into the studio]. The second morning of the shoot, somebody broke in through the toilets through a window.'

One element of the shoot confounded the girls. 'There was a deer in the studio because someone had the bright idea of featuring one in the video,' Mel B recalled with bewilderment in her memoir. She remembers exchanging confused glances with the other girls. 'What the fuck is that deer doing here?' they mumbled to one another. This four-legged co-star was on set to make a cameo in the big city, a slice of wildlife in radical contrast to the modern metropolis. It doesn't appear, however, until the final eight seconds of the video at the tail end of a lengthy instrumental outro. Many music channels would segue into the next video midway through the outro meaning the deer often didn't make it to air.

The Spice Girls released '2 Become 1' as a single on 16 December 1996, the timing of which confirmed that the girl group was gunning for a Christmas No. 1. The United Kingdom's music charts began in 1952 but landing a Christmas No. 1 wasn't a sought-after accolade until 1973 when the British public witnessed a full-scale showdown between Slade's 'Merry Xmas Everybody' and Wizzard's 'I Wish It Could Be Christmas Everyday'. This festive faceoff grew into a spectator sport and once bookies took notice it became an annual tradition to places bets on which song would nab the top spot. Analyst James Masterton explained in *The Guardian* why Christmas figures are especially meaningful. 'It took on a particular significance being number one at Christmas time because it meant you had the most popular record out at the very point when the most people were actually inside record stores,' James explained. Ultimately the Spice Girls triumphed, selling 462,000 copies of '2 Become 1' in the first week to claim their first Christmas No. 1. while making history in the process—the song remains the fastest selling single of all time by a girl group.

If there was any doubt about who 1996's breakout artist was, this settled it. At the year's close, all three singles released by the Spice Girls sat within the top five best-selling singles of the year. 'The Christmas

No. 1 is one of the most important records of the year and so we really felt like we'd achieved something,' Mel B noted in her memoir. 'We were overwhelmed. It felt like the whole world knew us now, which was a bit frightening.'

## 'Love Thing'
Duration: 3:38
Written by Spice Girls, Eliot Kennedy & Cary Baylis
Additional production and mix by Andy Bradfield
Recording engineer: Jeremy Wheatley
Assistant: Adam Brown
All instruments by Absolute
Additional programming by Paul Waller

'Love Thing' is an intensely autobiographical track, the writing of which triggered a lot of introspection for the Spice Girls about their individual journeys to self-prioritisation. 'When I sing this, I always think about how I was engaged before I got together with the girls. When I met them, I realised that it was all a mistake,' Victoria mused in her memoir. 'A great song—especially after what I'd just been through with [my ex-boyfriend]—full of lines about broken hearts and not going down that road again, and how my plans no longer include you, you loser,' Victoria snapped, clearly still heated. Upon joining the Spice Girls, Emma's love life followed a shockingly similar track to Victoria's. 'I also had a boyfriend and they helped me get rid of him,' she said. 'I was in a pretty bad relationship as well and he went out the window,' Mel C added candidly. 'We helped each other out to get what we wanted, and we gave each other strength.' In the second verse, when Mel C sings, 'You're not the only thing I've got on my mind', she's communicating loud and clear that her focus lies elsewhere.

The support system that existed within the band during this era was paramount to the eventual success of the Spice Girls, both as a band and as young women. With ambitious career objectives in mind, the Spice Girls were not willing to waste valuable time and energy doing the heavy lifting in imbalanced relationships. 'At that point in our lives boys and love were second to what we had as girls together and most of our early songs reflect that,' Mel B said. On the second day developing the track, Mel B and Geri composed a rap section that succinctly summarised this sentiment. 'God help the mister that comes between me and my sisters', they spit in unison—a lyric that nods to the song 'Sisters' written by

Irving Berlin for the 1954 film *White Christmas*. Ultimately 'Love Thing' posits that a dependent man shouldn't be able to hinder his girlfriend's personal growth and lyrics like, 'I've got some living to do, don't assume I'm gonna be with you' and 'I keep on giving still you're asking for more' are cutting and direct.

'The first song that we wrote with Eliot was "Love Thing",' Mel B later wrote. 'A far cry from the stuff that [Heart Management] wanted us to sing, it set a precedent for the Spice sound and message with its punchy melody and assertive lyrics. Eliot had already set down a beat for the song and sketched a melody; the rest came together in a kind of jam.' With the creation of 'Love Thing' at Eliot's home studio, the Spice Girls established an effortless professional relationship which further bloomed into a personal friendship. The day after their abrupt split from Heart Management, the band moved into Eliot Kennedy's Sheffield home and spent their days at work and in the evening, they'd change into pyjamas and watch *Star Trek* reruns together on the couch. 'It was something, all of a sudden having five young girls move into your house,' Eliot laughed. 'I lived on my own thank goodness, because I don't know if my partner would have been able to deal with it.'

In a fun fluke, the Spice Girls were back in Eliot's studio remastering 'Love Thing' exactly one year after they wrote the track together. Geri had noted the significance of the date and wanted to mark the occasion and acknowledge how far they'd come in just 12 months. She visited a jeweller's shop in downtown Sheffield and purchased five matching gold rings, each engraved with the word SPICE on the outside. The inside of each band was labelled 'one of five'. She returned to the studio to finish the post-production on 'Love Thing' and chose a quiet moment to present the symbolic rings to her bandmates. Photographs of the ring are featured prominently on the album artwork and CD disc design for *Spice*.

Manager Simon Fuller felt that 'Love Thing' was strong enough both musically and from a branding perspective to be the band's debut single, but the Spice Girls fought fervently for 'Wannabe' instead, insisting it better represented their band identity. It was a contender again during discussions about their second single but returned to the backburner in favour of 'Say You'll Be There'. The song was never released as a single.

## 'LAST TIME LOVER'
Duration: 4:11
Written by Spice Girls, Andy Watkins & Paul Wilson
Produced by Absolute

Mixed by Dave Way
Recording engineer: Al Stone
Assistant: Adam Brown
All instruments by Absolute
Additional programming by Dave Way and Statik
Additional background vocals by Eric Gooden

The heavy thumping R&B beat that opens 'Last Time Lover' signals a tonal shift at the midway point of *Spice*. If the slow and seductive rhythm wasn't enough to command listeners' attention, then the lustful wolf-whistle that pierces the arrangement certainly finishes the job. 'The whistle at the front of the track was performed by the sound engineer Al Stone as neither us nor the girls could do it convincingly,' revealed the Absolute production team.

'Last Time Lover' is the first song sequentially on *Spice* that was co-written by Paul Wilson and Andy Watkins, a writer-producer team known collectively as Absolute. Paul and Andy first met as students at the University of Bristol; Andy was a guitarist who performed in punk rock cover bands, whilst Paul was a classically trained musician fresh out of London's Royal College of Music. Although on the surface they seemed like a mismatched pair, their shared interest in funk, soul, and R&B birthed a symbiotic partnership. They received a government grant to establish their own small recording studio in Bath, where they began recording music and remixing dance tracks under the moniker Bristol Bass Line before moving to London together and rebranding as Absolute. They had just been signed to BMG's publishing department when the music company's creative director, Marc Fox, caught the Spice Girls' performance at their 1994 Nomis Studios talent showcase. He excitedly reached out to Paul and Andy. 'You won't believe it, but I've got your act,' he told them, kickstarting an invaluable songwriting partnership.

The concept for 'Last Time Lover' underwent a total reversal during the writing process. 'Initially we called it 'First Time Lover' and wrote it about losing your virginity,' Geri revealed. 'But we knocked that out.' Instead of romanticising a young woman's naiveté, the Spice Girls opted for an empowered approach. The track celebrates female confidence and experience while highlighting the double standard that means the sexual behaviour of men and women are judged on different moral rubrics. 'It's about how boys gossip saying, "Oh yeah, I had her last night and she did this and that",' Mel B said about the track in *Girl Power!* 'Well, we did our version of it. Basically, that I had him, he wasn't any good and

I want something better.' For Emma, it was about having the autonomy to make her own decisions. 'It's saying I'm not a floozy, I like choosing the right men,' she elaborated. In interviews, the Spice Girls were frank about the pitfalls of dating and preached a message of self-advocacy, a habit of the band that made them unconventional relationship gurus for their young fanbase. In the spring of 1997, this concept was even spun into an advice column in their *Spice Girls Official Magazine*—fans mailed handwritten letters to the Spice Girls' P.O. Box and the girls gave advice that balanced sincerity with personal anecdotes and goofy jokes, further endearing themselves to a generation of fans who felt as though, even if separated by a certain degree of fame and wealth, the Spice Girls were just like them. Geri's opening line of the song sets a simple and non-negotiable standard: 'Treat me right.'

'Last Time Lover' is the only track from their debut album to never be performed live.

## 'MAMA'
Duration: 5:04
Written by Spice Girls, Matt Rowe & Richard Stannard
Produced by Matt Rowe & Richard Stannard
Mixed by Dave Way & Absolute
Recording engineer: Adrian Bushby
Assistant: Patrick McGovern
Keyboards and programming by Matt Rowe & Richard Stannard
Guitar by Greg Lester
Cello by Tony Ward
Violin by Jackie Drew
Choir arranged by Mark Beswick
Released as a single on 3 March 1997

The Spice Girls always wanted to make music that centred strong female voices so a song honouring their mothers was an apropos addition to the Spice catalogue. 'Mel B had come up with the idea for us to write a song dedicated to our mums,' Mel C recounted in her memoir. 'At that point, she had been arguing with her mum, they were really going through it. I think she wanted to remind herself how important her mum was, how important they were and are to all of us.' Mel B later explained what was motivating her during this writing session. 'The sentiments are really that your mum's probably the best friend you've got,' she revealed in the band's *Girl Power!* book. 'Whether she's a bit of a landmine or just over-protective, she probably knows you better than you know yourself in some ways.' Each Spice Girl retreated to a private nook in the studio to reflect on the bond they shared with their own mother and craft their own personalised verse before reconvening to tackle to the chorus. Matt and Biff stitched the pieces together over a piano accompaniment but the band felt that things were sounding sparse. They also feared that the lyrics were cheesy and that perhaps they'd treaded too far into the realm of schmaltz. In a solution to both issues, Matt and Biff introduced heavier drums, filled out the early part of the track with a violin and cello based melody line, and arranged the song so that it crescendoed with a gospel choir harmonising behind a sonorous rendition of the chorus. The track was transformed from piddly to impressive, finally a worthy tribute to the women who raised them.

While conceptually clear-cut, the Spice Girls introduced a greater level of depth to the track by dismantling idealised visions of motherhood. A perfect mother is expected to be omnipresent to dote on her children—her kids are her whole world in a way that erodes her independent identity until the role of caregiver becomes the totality of her existence. 'Mama', however, is a song about a mother's love, not necessarily a mother's service. 'People ask where my girl power came from and I'd really have to say that, for me, I got my girl power from my mother,' Emma said in a 2001 *The People* interview. 'When I was younger, I remember seeing this woman who was still growing herself, still learning, and I thought, "That's how I want to be when I'm her age."' This understanding of mothers as autonomous and evolving individuals helps the song address the unconditional love of a parent rather than simply reading as a thank you note for domestic labour.

'Mama' also leans into the complexities of human relationships. Close mother-daughter relationships in art and media are often aspirational yet unattainable and feature caricatures who are totally in sync and free of conflict. But 'Mama' doesn't do that. From the beginning, listeners are shown relationships that have ups and downs, disagreements, and disappointments, but at no point do these imperfections negate the love between mother and daughter. This grounds the track and makes the song's concept infinitely more accessible while ensuring the sentimentality doesn't cross over into cloying territory. The song is about two generations experiencing growth—imperfect mothers who are still learning, and their daughters who are gaining perspective with age. 'I've had a lot of time to think about / About the way I used to be / Never had a sense of my responsibility', Mel B sings, showing a level of self-reflection that may have surprised critics who were only expecting bald declarations about girls running the world. 'It's all about how you're such a cow to your mum when you're going through that rebellious teenage stage,' Mel C said. 'Then, when you get a bit older, you realize that whatever she was doing, she was only doing it for your own good and you think, "Shit, I was really horrible!"' 'Mama' features five young women taking ownership of past mistakes and when Mel B sings, 'I didn't want to hear it then but I'm not ashamed to say it now / Every little thing you said and did was right for me', it acts as a gentle reminder to their young fanbase that growing up requires learning and changing.

'We already knew what the video would look like when we were writing the song,' Mel C said. 'We were all so family-oriented that we knew we wanted our mums to be a big part of the visuals.' The music video was filmed in a studio in Perivale, West London beginning on 15 January 1997. Once again, the Spice Girls were working with Big TV! directors Andy Delaney and Monty Whitebloom. This time, however, there were a few snags. '"Mama" went really badly wrong because we had this stupid idea really,' Andy recounted during an appearance on *90s Noise*. 'We were going to do this kind of kids TV show idea. First, the set was delayed and then a light fell off from the ceiling and nearly hit somebody. And so the video got kind of screwy. We didn't do any more [videos with the Spice Girls] after that.' An alternate edit of the video exists that leans more into this children's programming idea. It opens with the live studio audience chanting for the Spice Girls, each girl emerging theatrically on set as though the star of a sitcom. Geri and Emma speed onto the stage in a small flame-coloured convertible, Victoria and Mel B emerge from a set of double doors at the back of the stage and, arm in arm, strut to centre stage. Finally, Mel C descends onto the stage from the ceiling on a rope. 'That bit was never used, so braving those heights ended up being a waste of time. Thanks for that, everyone!' she quipped.

Although Andy and Monty felt that the video shoot went poorly, the Spice Girls only had positive things to say about the experience, in large part because they were delighted that their mums got to tag along. 'It was really good for our mums to see what we do—all the waiting around and getting ready,' Mel C remarked. Victoria concurred. 'It took a long time to film it, but it was nice that our mums were there and could see what we're doing,' she said in *Girl Power!* 'They were actually knackered at the end of the day, and I said to my mum, "Ha! Now you know how I feel every day!"' Geri also enjoyed having her mum around but found it highlighted the bizarreness of a job in entertainment. 'If you worked in Sainsbury's, you wouldn't get your mum to sit with you on the till,' she teased. Performance footage of the Spice Girls perched atop stools on stage is intercut with their real childhood photos—a sea of chubby cheeks and toothy smiles prove that these larger-than-life popstars were once just like the children seated in the audience. Each Spice Girl gets a moment in the spotlight to serenade her mother in a show of gratitude. There are also snippets of footage stylised to look like old home movies in which five little girls (their signature Spice styles already in full force) play, dance, and sing together. These segments feature young actresses and while this footage may have only been included for narrative purposes, it may have also been a subtle rewriting of history that set the Spice Girls' origin story in girlhood instead of at auditions in 1994. The band was growing tired of being dismissed as manufactured pop.

'It was a bit much, I had to think about the video, make sure I looked good, pay attention to the fans, and look after my mum—all at the same time!' Emma said, clearly finding the two-day shoot a demanding one. And she wasn't the only Spice Girl who found the experience emotionally taxing. During a short break from filming, Mel C was approached by an assistant. Mel's father was on the phone, and it was urgent. 'I've got something to tell you,' he said down the line. 'You know how you've always wanted a sister? Well, you've got one. She's actually just a few years younger than you.' The news stunned Mel. 'My dad had fathered a girl years before, but the relationship hadn't worked out and he hadn't kept in touch,' Mel recounted in her memoir. '[A] tabloid paper got hold of the story and basically said to my dad, either you tell her or we will.' Finishing the video shoot while trying to digest such shocking news was a challenge for Mel and she wasn't afforded much privacy in the days that followed either. 'It was so intense, and our lives were so bizarre. [T]here was this press intrusion but that was the way it was, and you had to deal with it,' she reflected during a 2020 appearance on *Desert Island Discs*. 'When I met my sister, a newspaper was actually there, and they photographed us and interviewed us and when I think about that now I just think... What? Why on earth did I agree to that and why did anybody allow me to do that? It's insane.' Only with distance was she able to see how harmful and unsustainable it was to live under a microscope. 'That was my normal everyday life, that I would have a tabloid newspaper just follow me around to do something really personal and heart wrenching.'

The Spice Girls released the double A-side 'Mama'/'Who Do You Think You Are' single on 3 March 1997. It debuted at No. 1 on Mother's Day on 15 March 1997 and has remained a touching Mother's Day staple since. During the 2007 Return of the Spice Girls tour the group frequently turned their performance of the song into a family affair by inviting their young families on stage. Only Mel C was child-free at this time, so special guests included Victoria's three sons Brooklyn, Romeo and Cruz; Mel B's two daughters Phoenix and Angel; Geri's daughter Bluebell; and Emma's son Beau. In a sweet, full-circle moment the Spice Girls revisited a song they had written from a child's perspective, now having transitioned into motherhood themselves.

Upon release some music critics found 'Mama' too saccharine and lacking in the Spice Girls' trademark moxie however many saw this gentler side of the band and their barefaced display of emotion endearing. Ken Tucker of *Entertainment Weekly* called the song 'a fearlessly corny ballad'. Beyond the commercial success of the track, 'Mama' holds a special place in the Spice Girls' hearts for sentimental reasons. 'It seems really silly but every time I sing "Mama" I cry,' Emma shared in a 1997 interview. 'We did it at the Royal Albert Hall for the film and I was looking up at my mum and crying, because it was about us. It was quite an emotional moment. I think it will always affect me that way.'


## 'WHO DO YOU THINK YOU ARE'
Duration: 4:00
Written by Spice Girls, Andy Watkins & Paul Wilson
Produced by Absolute
Mixed by Dave Way
Recording engineer: Jeremy Wheatley
Assistant: Adam Brown
All instruments by Absolute
Additional background vocals by Mary Pearce
Released as a single 3 March 1997


When the Spice Girls began working on 'Who Do You Think You Are' with Absolute's Andy Watkins and Paul Wilson they had two objectives: they wanted to write a song about their experiences in the music industry and they wanted that song to feel like a party. And thus, a dance-pop banger about industry pitfalls was born. A fully fleshed-out single came into view in a solitary session which helped Andy and Paul better understand what was so special about the group—the Spice Girls could conceptualise an entire number from lyrics to marketing through to choreography. The song was recorded in London's Olympic Studios and had few vocal alterations made in post-production. 'Because of the fact we were not using computers, we had to work them very hard,' Paul remembered. 'They were in that recording booth for hours because we just had to get the right take.'

From inception, the Spice Girls had clashed with the suit-wearing executives who held the keys to the industry. Boy bands were given the opportunity to flourish because labels saw them as a lucrative pull for young female fans; girl bands were contrastingly seen as obsolete. The Spice Girls knew that this was misguided. 'We wrote "Who Do You Think You Are" as a response to all these men trying to order us about,' Mel C extrapolated in her memoir. 'The more people told us what we should and shouldn't do, the more it solidified who we were and what we wanted to be. You're telling US what young girls want? We ARE young women, we might have a bit more insight than you,' she railed. 'By that point, "Never lose your soul, never lose control", was firmly ingrained in us,' she concluded, citing the song's resonant lyrics. The band also wanted to address that artists and performers could perpetuate similarly toxic behaviours once they'd found success in the industry. 'I loved writing that song because I feel [it's] the absolute embodiment of what fame is about,' Geri reflected in the 2007 documentary *Spice Girls: Giving You Everything*. 'The race is on to get out of the bottom. It's saying I want to get out of where I'm living right now, and I want to make it to the top. And then on your way to the top, are you going to lose who you are?' When egos run amok, admirable traits like ambition and determination can quickly shapeshift into arrogance and entitlement. 'It's saying, look, you've really lost the plot,' Mel C said. 'What do you think you're doing? You're so caught up in this celebrity world.'

On 10 February 1997, the Spice Girls began an ambitious two-day shoot led by director Gregg Masuak in London's Willesden area—over the next 48 hours they would be creating three different video versions of 'Who Do You Think You Are'. On the first day of the shoot, the Spice Girls performed on an LED-tiled dancefloor that cast a brilliant white glow on a crowd of club-goers partying at the foot of the stage. The band also filmed segments in small, boxy rooms decorated with bold colours and textured patterns. 'There were loads of freaky extras—jugglers and fire eaters and weirdo people,' Mel C recollected in *Girl Power!*. 'We shot it at a really mad club—a real dive. The bogs were horrible and we had to have our makeup done in a Winnebago. The vibe was excellent though—I think it was my favourite video because it was such good fun.' From this first day of footage emerged two versions of the video, one that leaned more heavily into the wild and wacky extras and one that was centred on the band's performance.

The group had a slightly delayed start the next morning when Geri required a hospital visit to have one of her false nails dislodged from her ear after it popped off during an ill-fated scratch. This of course made headlines, as was typical for any minor incident involving the Spice Girls during this era. 'Spice Girl Gets Nail-ed!' screamed one *MTV* headline. 'Halliwell was immediately rushed to the casualty ward of Central Middlesex Hospital where she was treated and released with no permanent damage to her ear.' With a crisis averted the second and final day of filming went ahead as planned.

'Who Do You Think You Are' was the official Comic Relief single of 1997 and so the shoot on 11 February 1997 was dedicated entirely to producing a Red Nose Day video featuring some very special guests. Christened the Sugar Lumps, an alternate universe version of the Spice Girls took shape with some famous faces transforming into the fab five: Kathy Burke portrayed Sporty Spice, Dawn French was Posh Spice, Llewella Gideon was Scary Spice, Lulu was Baby Spice, and Jennifer Saunders transformed into Ginger Spice. 'When you'd turn round to talk to Victoria it would be Dawn French,' Mel C said of the disorienting doppelgangers. The comedians committed fully to their popstar roles with Dawn lurching about the set on towering stilettos to channel her inner Posh Spice. It was a strange experience for the girls to see their personality quirks amplified in the name of parody. 'The freakiest thing about it was seeing Jennifer Saunders,' Geri recalled in her autobiography. 'She looked just like me and everyone said they thought she was me. It was absolutely bizarre—the makeup, everything. It was scary.' The resulting video is a cheerful performance of 'Who Do You Think You Are' that mixes the Sugar Lumps in with the Spice Girls. 'Sometimes there would be four of us, and a fake Posh or a fake Scary,' Geri laughed. 'In the editing suite, they cut the film around and created a wonderfully bizarre performance.' After the video shoot, the girls stayed in contact with Jennifer Saunders who appeared again in *Spice World The Movie* and wrote the script for the group's 2012 West End jukebox musical, *Viva Forever!*

It's impossible to examine the cultural impact of 'Who Do You Think You Are' without acknowledging the Spice Girls' decade-defining performance of the song at the 1997 BRIT Awards. A couple weeks before the event, a Virgin-appointed stylist presented Geri with a black Gucci minidress as a wardrobe option for the fast-approaching ceremony. Geri was drawn to its sexy silhouette, reminiscent of a 1950s one-piece bathing suit. While the dress itself was nice, she felt that a jet-black piece of fabric was too boring to wear on Britain's biggest stage.

The Spice Girls had attended the 1996 BRITs as unknowns and now, just one year later, they were the hottest act in pop. Playing it safe would be a missed opportunity.

With five days to go until the BRIT awards, Geri had the idea to emblazon the dress with a large Union Jack. She did a quick sketch of what she was visualizing, grabbed the black mini dress and hightailed it to the home of her stepsister who was a more skilled seamstress. Geri had a vague recollection that in some countries desecrating a flag was a crime, so to avoid tarnishing a national symbol she grabbed a £5 Union Jack tea towel to stitch to the front of the dress. Geri was aware of the flag's colonial connotations as well as some ugliness in the flag's recent history and was worried that her patriotism could be mistaken for nationalism—in the 1970s the flag had been co-opted by neo-Nazis and the National Front, a right-wing extremist party who stoked xenophobia in the name of British supremacy. To ensure that her messaging was positive and inclusive, she decided to add a large white peace sign to the back of the dress, specifically a Campaign for Nuclear Disarmament symbol. In addition to clarifying her intent, the peace sign felt like a cohesive extension of the Spice Girls' existing motifs since they had a habit of flashing V-signs with their hands in the name of peace and girl power. Karen sewed up the crotch so that the lining of the dress was enclosed—the exceptionally short dress displayed several inches of Geri's knickers. As a final touch, Geri grabbed a pair of platform boots and painted them fire engine red with a can of car spray that her mechanic father had left in the garage before his passing a few years prior. The look was complete; it was scrappy and unorthodox, but Geri liked it. And she hoped others would too.

The BRIT Awards were held on 24 February 1997 at the Earls Court Exhibition Centre in London and the Spice Girls were tasked with kicking off proceedings with the night's big opening number. While the band had already established a dance routine for the track, they spent two days refining it for the global stage with famed choreographer Priscilla Samuels—thousands of fans would be watching from the audience while 30 million viewers tuned in around the world. The Spice Girls stood with their backs turned to the audience, breathlessly awaiting their music cue while a massive screen rolled glamorous pre-taped footage of them as a backdrop. 'As we stood there in our silhouetted positions before the curtains went up and the music started, we all felt an enormous buzz,' Mel B later wrote of the high-pressure moment in her 2002 memoir. '[W]e weren't holding hands like we usually did at the beginning of a set. We couldn't turn round and look at each other as we so often did. We had to stand stock still like statues. Little did we know as we waited for the music to start that we were creating an iconic image of Girl Power.' When an abridged version of 'Wannabe' blared the girls turned to the audience and strutted to centre stage where the funky opening guitar groove of 'Who Do You Think You Are' began with a zing. The Spice Girls launched into their high energy routine stomping, spinning, and swivelling their hips. There were no elaborate set pieces, no phalanx of backup dancers, no pyrotechnics. Just five girls showcasing one of the tenets of Spice: they were having a blast. 'It made me feel really proud that we were doing a dance we'd made up in a tiny little beaten-up recording studio in front of all those people and cameras,' Geri later reminisced. 'We had that dance routine almost from the moment we wrote "Who Do You Think You Are"—the very same routine that you saw us doing on the BRITs.' Years later, Mel C attempted to summarise the wave of emotions the group experienced in that moment. 'After months, years, of hard work, we had reached the pinnacle of our success, and what a moment it was,' she said. 'We came flying off the stage after our BRITs performance, laughing, hugging and crying.'

The night was only just beginning for the Spice Girls who would end up taking home two awards. Geri changed out of her Union Jack mini dress and into a shimmering red strapless gown for the awards portion of the evening. 'That morning I'd [had] the corset fitted to make my waist look smaller,' she explained. 'I also bought a basque to wear under the dress [and] I discovered that it actually made the dress slip down when I walked and I had to keep tugging it up.' While accepting the award for British Video of the Year an impassioned Geri thrust her arm above her head and her top plunged, flashing the audience.

In a February 1997, *Vanity Fair* interview, Oasis frontman Liam Gallagher said that, despite being nominated, he would not be attending the BRITs. 'If I bump into the Spice Girls, I will smack them,' he explained bitterly. Writer David Kamp dedicated a sizable portion of the article to disparaging the girl group. 'The Spice Girls, a quintet of latter-day dolly birds whose music is a forgettable mix of anodyne lite-funk and MOR balladry, have become pop sensations by projecting an image that is at once sexy and laddish, talking about 'shagging' and football while wearing virtually no clothing.' When the Spice Girls triumphed over Oasis in the British Single of the Year category, Mel C took the opportunity to address Liam's threats of violence by challenging the singer in her acceptance speech. 'Liam, come and have a go if you think you're hard enough!'

The 1997 BRIT Awards belonged to the Spice Girls in every meaningful way—between their sizzling 'Who Do You Think You Are' performance, an iconic fashion moment, their multiple wins, a public spat with a mouthy rock star, and Geri's nip-slip, the group had dominated all public discourse about the high-profile event. In a piece commemorating the 20th anniversary of the performance, Samuel McManus for *Attitude Magazine* reflected on the impact of this moment. 'This single performance would go on to become one of the defining images of '90s "Cool Britannia,"' he wrote. 'The performance still ranks as one of the greatest moments in British pop history.' A pun on the patriotic naval anthem 'Rule Britannia', the term 'Cool Britannia' referred to a celebration of '90s youth culture in Britain that harkened back to the 1960s when the signature Britishness of cultural exports, from The Beatles to Twiggy, were lauded as evidence of British excellence. The artistic output of the UK during the 1990s was often proudly and distinctly British—edgy indie cinema like Danny Boyle's *Trainspotting* helped legitimise the nation's reinvigorated film scene while designer Alexander McQueen's theatricality captured the attention of the fashion world. Under the umbrella of Britpop, bands like Oasis, Blur, Suede, and Pulp made alternative rock stylish and mainstream. While the Spice Girls were still viewed as a mass market outlier in this trendy scene, the image of Geri in her Union Jack dress made her a poster child of the movement.

With a week to go before the single's 3 March 1997 release, 'Who Do You Think You Are' was already at the apex of pop music discussions everywhere. The track received favourable reviews and upon release became the Spice Girls' fourth consecutive No. 1 single in the United Kingdom. The Spice Girls were the first act to nab four No. 1s with their first four singles and this coup only heightened interest in their debut album which was fast approaching sales of 20 million. The band's profile had already been on the rise, but the BRITs pushed them to the next level. 'There are certain moments in your life that you remember forever,' Victoria reminisced in her memoir. 'There aren't many of them that stay as important and as vivid as they were at the time. This one did.'

## 'SOMETHING KINDA FUNNY'
Duration: 4:05
Written by Spice Girls, Andy Watkins & Paul Wilson
Produced by Absolute
Mixed by Dave Way
Recording engineer: Jeremy Wheatley
Assistant: Adam Brown
All instruments by Absolute

'The first song we did with [Absolute] was "Something Kinda Funny",' Victoria recalled in her memoir. In early 1995, the girl group embarked on a journey deep into Southwest London to meet Andy Watkins and Paul Wilson, growing wearier with each passing mile. They looped through endless roundabouts, crossed narrow bridges, and traversed an unwelcoming industrial district that was packed with cold manufacturing plants and smoke-billowing factories while exchanging unsavoury rumours they'd heard about the area. Upon their arrival at Absolute headquarters on Tagg's Island they found a shed-sized studio packed to the gills with equipment. In David Sinclair's *Wannabe: How The Spice Girls Reinvented Pop*, Paul and Andy laughed recalling their first encounter with the band. 'They came in and just sexually harassed us for the first hour or so,' Andy chuckled. 'They definitely bewitched you. It was a case of by all means necessary to win you over. But they did it in a natural way. You were allowed to join in their gang for a small amount of time.'

Although their personalities gelled, there were some creative differences at the outset. 'They played us a few [of their] tracks which we didn't particularly like,' Andy sighed. Paul had the same fears. 'When they started to sing, it was never quite right from our point of view,' he shared. 'It was always very poptastic.' Absolute wanted to make soulful music whereas the Spice Girls, despite being interested in soul, seemed hardwired for pop. 'Paul and Andy were more old-school soul than Matt and Biff,' Mel B elaborated about the pair. 'They were into more of a funk vibe—more Angie Stone than Bananarama.' When the girls played Absolute their demo of 'Wannabe', spirits went from bad to worse. 'We listened to it and we just didn't get it at all,' Paul said. 'It was so different to what we were doing. We thought how's this going to work? We're not the right people to be doing this band.' In a last-ditch effort, they decided to throw away any preconceived notions of genre or mood and just write from a blank slate. That's when things began to take shape. 'Something Kinda Funny' was the first Spice Girls song that future manager Simon Fuller heard after Andy and Paul passed a rough demo along through their shared manager.

'Something Kinda Funny' is a smooth midtempo number that marries the Spice Girls' pop tendencies with a generous helping of soul. 'It's about how there must have been something kinda funny going on with us lot, and how it was fate that we all met up,' Emma said of the song's inspiration. The track is a harmonic feast that exemplifies the band's vocal strengths, building to a conclusion where Emma's crisp vocal riffs soar above the chorus, the other girls' voices contrasting beautifully over a bouncy bassline. 'I get so angry when I hear people say that the Spice Girls can't sing,' griped Pepi Lemer, noted jazz singer and original Spice Girls vocal coach, in Sinclair's *Wannabe: How The Spice Girls Reinvented Pop*. 'I cannot bear that put-down, because I know differently. When you listen to those songs you hear each individual voice—the depth of Geri's voice, the lightness of Emma's voice, the soulful sound of the two Mels—you can always identify their sound. Of course they can sing.'

## 'Naked'
Duration: 4:25
Written by Spice Girls, Andy Watkins & Paul Wilson
Produced by Absolute
Mixed by Al Stone and Absolute
Engineered by Al Stone
Assisted by Adam Brown
All instruments by Absolute
Additional background vocals by Mary Pearce

'Naked' is the most mysterious offering on the Spice Girls' debut album but despite its hint of darkness Paul Wilson from Absolute recalled its writing session being fresh and fun. '"Naked" was one of the first songs we recorded,' he recalled. 'Geri decided she wanted to do her vocals lying down, so we had to set the mic up on the floor.' Her raspy delivery, sometimes bordering on spoken-word, lent itself to the track's shadowy tone. 'It's a weird track,' Mel B reflected. 'We were thinking about what it's like when you walk into a room and everybody stops and looks, as though you've got no clothes on. We've all had that in one way or another.' As young women, the Spice Girls had all been on the receiving end of objectifying gazes but once the band ascended to fame and captured the attention of the intrusive tabloid press these violations grew in severity and frequency. Written in their pre-fame days, 'Naked' is oddly prophetic.

At the height of their fame the Spice Girls were treated like public property and violated without hesitation. Photographers sometimes crouched in the road to snap upskirt shots as the Spice Girls exited vehicles, with one paparazzo even forcing his camera up Victoria's skirt during a particularly unpleasant visit to BBC Radio 1. 'The paparazzi behaved like pigs all day,' Geri later remarked with disgust. The harassment was brazen and it was constant. While vacationing in Gran Canaria, Geri and Mel B befriended a couple who later sold their holiday photos to a paper. During another outing, Emma and her mother were photographed while swimming together. The purposely unflattering shot framed them from behind and the photos were run in the paper under headlines asking the reader to identify which one was the Spice Girl, a nasty jab at the size of Emma's bum. Soon morning TV programs and radio stations were analysing Emma's body under a microscope. 'That was so horrible,' she later said of the incident. 'It was really hard to get over, especially because my mum was involved in it as well. People can be horrible.' Geri comforted a crying Emma as the photos spread. 'Quite rightly, there was an enormous backlash against *The Mirror* for publishing the shot of Emma and her mother,' Geri recalled in her memoir. 'Women, in particular, were outraged. Why should a twenty-year-old be scrutinised in such a way? No wonder we have so many young girls with eating disorders.' Unsurprisingly, many of the Spice Girls struggled with their body image—Geri, Mel C, and Victoria all spoke openly later about the disordered eating they engaged in to meet beauty standards at this time. '[Newspapers] would cheerfully berate those who put on weight but then reprimand those who'd lost too much weight. You literally could not win,' Mel C reflected in her 2022 memoir. 'This didn't only affect those being talked about, it sent out such damaging messages to the women reading this rubbish too. It was such a harmful time.'

Around this time Victoria confessed to the other girls that she didn't discuss anything substantial during personal phone calls because she had an unshakeable feeling that her lines were tapped; she then learned that the other four girls were exercising the same caution. Less than a decade later, investigations that brought the *News of the World*'s phone hacking scandal to light would prove this was not paranoia at all but a healthy distrust of an immoral industry. Tabloids were listening in on the private conversations of celebrities, politicians, and even just everyday people who had experienced tragedy. There were no boundaries that the press wouldn't cross for profit and the Spice Girls were a cash cow. 'It was said that a Spice Girls front page could increase daily sales by 10 percent,' Geri recalled.

Geri endured a public shaming in the autumn of 1996 when photos of her in various states of undress surfaced from her pre-Spice glamour modelling days. After *News of the World* ran a story in October 1996 with the headline 'Spice Girl's Nude Photo Shock', Geri entered a hellish period. 'From that moment on every glamour photographer, studio and picture library in the country began searching their archives for topless or nude shots of Geri Halliwell,' she later said. Photos were subsequently printed in paper after paper. When an inconsiderate journalist in Oslo, Norway thrust a naked photo in Geri's face mid-interview she tried to stay composed. 'It is something I did,' she said carefully. 'As we point out in 'Wannabe' if you want to know me now, forget my past.' While the inspiration for 'Naked' stemmed from the sensation of being vulnerable and exposed, the band couldn't have imagined how literal this would become as they were flayed on the world stage.

In early live performances of 'Naked', the Spice Girls emerged onstage in dark cloaks and ambled to five backwards chairs at centre stage, discarding their wraps and taking a seat unclothed. They performed the moody number shielded by the back of the chair with only their bare limbs suggestively exposed. Those seated in the audience could only see what the group intentionally revealed; the routine was a clear reclamation of their own boundaries. The number's styling referenced a famous photoshoot from 1963 featuring model Christine Keeler, who posed nude while straddling a plywood chair, the chair's back protecting her modesty. While the image immortalised a movement, it also encouraged discussion about how sexual liberation could be weaponised to exploit women after it was learned that Christine Keeler was pressured into stripping off for the shoot. 'Christine was reluctant to do so, but the producers insisted, saying that it was written in her contract,' said photographer Lewis Morley in an interview with *V&A*. He proposed using the chair as a buffer to appease the producers while ensuring Christine was more comfortable with the nudity. The chairs used in both Christine's shoot and the Spice Girls' performance of 'Naked' were designed by Arne Jacobsen and have tapered backs that create a visual waistline. Allusions to this famous photoshoot draw parallels between the model and the girl group—there is a fine line between an empowered display of female sexuality and exploitation and the distinction is largely dependent on who has the decision-making power.

The staging of 'Naked' became a fixation with journalists and the Spice Girls were routinely questioned in interviews about whether they were truly nude. Victoria dryly stated that they were wearing fig leaves while the other girls played it coy and, with a wink, said they couldn't reveal their secrets. In reality, they were sporting flesh coloured body stockings to ensure there were no live mishaps. 'Showing characteristic shrewdness, the members of the group kept their hints of sexuality tame enough not to alienate their core female audience, but with their nudity-tease performance of the slow, sultry "Naked", they offered just enough raunch to placate those raging male hormones in the house,' wrote

Gilbert Garcia of the *Phoenix New Times* in his August 1998 concert review. The song's performance was prefaced by an intro featuring audio from Joel Schumacher's 1995 film *Batman Forever*. 'Relax. Tell me your dreams, tell me your fantasies, tell me your secrets, tell me your deepest, darkest fears', a robotic female voice announces over the arena's sound system, lines spoken in the film by a mind reading piece of technology called The Box. Midway through the live arrangement, the song samples the film again, this time using audio of the Riddler's low growls performed by comedian Jim Carrey.

Despite the song's mysterious air, the number became a source of fun for the band on tour. '"Naked" was the worst song for getting the giggles,' Mel B remarked in her memoir. The routine required the Spice Girls to look dramatically to their left or right every third beat and locking eyes with a bandmate would send the girls into fits of laughter. 'I sat next to Emma and every time we came face to face, we'd burst out laughing,' Mel B recalled fondly. 'We tried to avoid looking at each other, but it never seemed to work. We'd end up giggling our socks off. You had to grit your teeth, so you didn't smile because it was such a serious song. Even worse, the big screens showed close-ups of our faces throughout the whole song, so you really couldn't blow it.' The song was retired from their live shows upon the conclusion of the 1998 tour.

## 'IF U CAN'T DANCE'
Duration: 3:48
Written by Spice Girls, Matt Rowe & Richard Stannard
Produced by Matt Rowe & Richard Stannard
Mixed by Dave Way
Recording engineer: Adrian Bushby
Assistant: Patrick McGovern
Keyboards and programming by Matt Rowe & Richard Stannard
Backing vocals by Richard Stannard

'If U Can't Dance' closes out the Spice Girls' multi-platinum debut album with a repetitive and mesmerizing chorus that extols the virtue of dance skills. 'This one's about when you go to a club and you see a really good-looking bloke who seems really nice, and then you go to dance and it's "Oh no! What's going on?"' Victoria elaborated in *Girl Power!*. For Geri, however, the song wasn't as literal, with dancing ability really a metaphor for the truth that lies beneath a superficial exterior. 'It's about having preconceptions about people,' Geri said. 'Someone might look a certain way, but then when you meet them, they're completely the opposite of what you expected.' The track samples the backing groove from 'The Humpty Dance' by American hip hop group Digital Underground, as well as the saxophone hook from 'It's Just Begun' by The Jimmy Castor Bunch. 'If U Can't Dance' is a dance-pop track at its core but incorporates elements of hip hop, with Mel B rapping the opening verse: 'Now we got the flavour, the bad behaviour, the rhythm, the melody, the juice for you to savour.' Working alongside Matt and Biff again, the Spice Girls kept the song fun and timely. 'I love the lyric "there is never a Keanu but a dweeb",' laughed Mel C. The song was written in 1995 after films *Point Break* and *Speed* established actor Keanu Reeves as a '90s sex symbol.

The song's second verse is performed by Geri in Spanish. Her mother was born and raised near the historic city of Huesca in Northeast Spain before emigrating to England when she was 21. Geri was exposed to the language growing up but her grasp on the language wasn't perfect. 'I'm absolutely not fluent,' she clarified in a 2016 piece in *The Guardian*. 'But I could have a conversation if we were lost and you needed a beer.' For this reason, the English translation of Geri's verse is a little tricky to follow:

> Hey man, I saw you the other day
> It made me very, very happy
> Listen to the music, oh my goodness!
> Hey boy, you don't have anything
> What a scare, what a Swede, what a cock, how stiff!
> Oh don't touch me, oh what an ugly dog!
> Come, come, march out
> Take that music you sing to me quickly
> Be careful, be careful, hey boy, how crazy
> Take my rhythm, I'm going with you
> Hey man, I love a man, I need, yes
> But not you, a man, hey man
> Hey man, if you can't dance to this, you can't do nothing for me

'If U Can't Dance' was selected as the big opening number for the Spice Girls' two promotional shows in Istanbul, Turkey in October 1997 as well as on their subsequent 1998 Spiceworld Tour. 'The music to "If U Can't Dance" was playing, slowly building up in volume until the crowd was at a fever pitch,' Geri wrote about the tour's exhilarating opening night in Dublin, Ireland. 'The screen in front of us consisted of two massive doors that slid back as if they were part of a spaceship.' The doors slowly opened and the Spice Girls emerged, strutting forward in synchronised, robotic steps. 'It's a slamming routine,' Mel B said, proud of what they'd choreographed with the help of Priscilla Samuels. Their gruelling rehearsal schedule paid off and the number went off without a hitch. The live musical arrangement was an electrifying start to the show that leaned into a big rock sound with wailing guitars and a robust rhythm section.

After Geri's departure from the Spice Girls in May 1998, the group continued performing the number on their 1998 tour with a recording of Geri's Spanish section played over the venue's sound system while the remaining four Spice Girls used the interval for a dance break.

2

# Non-Album Tracks
# 1996–1997

'BUMPER TO BUMPER'
Duration: 3:43
Written by Spice Girls, Andy Watkins, Paul Wilson & Cathy Dennis
Produced by Absolute
Mixed by Absolute
Released as a B-side with 'Wannabe' on 8 July 1996

'Give way I'm comin' through', the Spice Girls bellow in the chorus of 'Bumper to Bumper', an apt warning of the group's impending rise to fame paired with the band's debut single. This B-side is a camp jaunt garnished with silly voices and honking horns that epitomises the band's tightrope walk between meticulous planning and impulsive risk taking. The track makes clear that whatever the band lacked in technical precision, they more than made up for with frolic and fun. Due to the overwhelming commercial success of 'Wannabe', Cathy Dennis, who co-wrote the B-side, saw a bountiful influx of royalty payments. 'Bumper to Bumper' was her first major songwriting credit and while the song was wholly overshadowed by its powerhouse A-side, it marked the beginning of her own prosperous career.

In 1986, a 17-year-old Cathy arrived in London to pursue a music career and was discovered by future Spice Girls manager, Simon Fuller. She signed with 19 Management and featured on the D-Mob club hit 'C'mon & Get My Love' and released three albums as a solo artist, yielding a handful of hits before re-evaluating her career goals and deciding that performing wasn't her passion. She wasn't, however, ready to abandon music entirely. '[I]t made sense to write for other people, where I would still have the freedom to be anyone I wanted to be on any given day, as a writer,' she said, 'so that I could still indulge myself creatively'. She began writing for Simon Fuller's assemblage of artists and penned 'Bumper to Bumper' with the then-unknown girl group over the course of two sessions at her home in Kingston. Watching the Spice Girls skyrocket to success with her friend's help was the inspiration she needed. 'I saw how, through Simon's genius, he shaped the Spice Girls. Nobody could have predicted the kind of success that he would be able to bring to that,' she said. 'I'd had the chance to write for them. At the time, I was still finishing being an artist, really. I saw these other writers experiencing huge success and as an ambitious career woman I wanted to be successful.' After Simon was fired by the Spice Girls, Cathy became heavily involved in the development of material for his new project, S Club 7. She went on to have an illustrious career, penning international hits like 'I Kissed a Girl' for Katy Perry, 'Can't Get You Out of My Head' for Kylie Minogue, and 'Toxic' for Britney Spears.

Cathy's affection for the girl group has only bloomed since their early collaboration. 'I love the Spice Girls, you know you can't not love the Spice Girls if you are a girl,' she gushed in a 2018 interview. When asked if she would work with them again in the event of a reunion she didn't hesitate: 'I would definitely embrace that opportunity if asked.'


'TAKE ME HOME'
Duration: 4:07
Written by Spice Girls, Andy Watkins & Paul Wilson
Produced by Absolute
Mixed by Absolute
Released as a B-side with 'Say You'll Be There' on 14 October 1996

The moodier counterpart to its synthpop A-side pairing, 'Take Me Home' is an atmospheric and understated rumination on what awaits beyond mundanity. It kicks off with a foreboding hum of strings that are pierced by a saxophone, the blasts fading into an echo. Over a minimalist R&B beat, a spoken-word intro is delivered by Geri: 'There's no mainstream, there's no happy medium, there's no in-between.' The track has a moody tone that uses the group's contrasting vocal abilities to its advantage— Victoria and Mel B lay the foundation with their lower registers while Mel C and Emma provide a necessary lift to counterbalance. Geri has another cryptic spoken word section at the song's close, bookending the number with mystique.

'ONE OF THESE GIRLS'
Duration: 3:33
Written by Spice Girls, Andy Watkins & Paul Wilson
Produced by Absolute
Mixed by Absolute
Released as a B-side with '2 Become 1' on 16 December 1996

After writing 'One of These Girls' with their Absolute cohort, the Spice Girls performed the number acapella prior to the release of *Spice*, mostly notably during their first major TV appearance on MTV's *Hanging Out* on 17 April 1996. Their acapella version was a faster, more playful interpretation that eliminated the somewhat stock verses and emphasised the harmonised, galloping chorus and breakdown. There is an obvious joy in the way they belt it out together live, racing eagerly to reach each new line. The recorded version is littered with squealing electronic flourishes and dependably celebrates female individuality while simultaneously 'giving lots of cheek and attitude' as the Spice Girls were wont to do.

'SLEIGH RIDE'
Duration: 3:18
Written by Leroy Anderson & Mitchell Parish
Produced by Matt Rowe & Richard Stannard
Mixed by Matt Rowe & Richard Stannard
Released as a B-side with '2 Become 1' on 16 December 1996

A spicy cover of 'Sleigh Ride' was included as the B-side to the Spice Girls' first Christmas No. 1 and while the musical arrangement remains faithful to the many covers that preceded it, the girl group's interpretation delivers a heavy helping of their signature offering: playful banter.

'This is definitely my most favourite time of the year,' Emma chirps, kicking off a relaxed exchange about the holidays with her bandmates. 'Oh yeah, mine too, yes, I think it is,' Mel B quickly agrees. 'I reckon Christmas is all right 'cause, like, the football season is still on and you can watch football on Boxing Day when everyone is being really boring and you're fed up of your presents,' Mel C interjects. A mere six months after the band's debut the public's grasp on the personalities of the Spice Girls was already so strong that simply slapping snippets of conversation on top of a cover was enough to entertain the masses. 'Well, what I say this Christmas is just do what you want but make sure you do it like a lady!' Victoria adds playfully. 'If you can't be good, be careful' cautions

Geri. 'And make sure you get all your pressies off Santa!' Mel C cries as the jingling music kicks in amidst the other girls' laughter.

This Christmas standard was originally written by American composer Leroy Anderson in 1946 with lyrics following in 1950 by Mitchell Parish for a version performed by the Andrews Sisters. The track subsequently found new life when The Ronettes covered it in 1963. In his 2004 book about the life and career of Leroy Anderson, biographer Steve Metcalf touched on the timeless and ever-shifting nature of the track, remarking, '"Sleigh Ride" [...] has been performed and recorded by a wider array of musical artists than any other piece in the history of Western music.' The Spice Girls were merely participating in a rite of passage by adding their version to the global songbook.

After a couple of verses the girls pop back in with another exchange. 'Remember to go to sleep on Christmas Eve otherwise Santa won't come,' Mel C warns. 'Father Christmas doesn't exist, Mel!' Victoria yells, an interesting addition to the song given that their primary audience was school-aged children. The other Spice Girls loudly shush Victoria and promise the listener that he does exist. 'We know 'cause we went to Lapland and we saw him,' Mel C says, referencing the group's recent highly publicised trip to a tourist destination in Northern Finland known to be Santa's official hometown. After another round of verbal sparring the group launches into a final verse, cheerfully harmonising their refrains of 'Ring-a-ling-a-ling-a-ding-dong-ding' before sending well wishes to fans. 'Good Tidings we bring to you and your schwing, we wish you a Merry Christmas and a Happy New Year', they shout enthusiastically, squeezing in what is likely a reference to the 1992 comedy film *Wayne's World* starring Mike Myers and Dana Carvey as basement-dwelling public access TV personalities. Whether pre-scripted or not, the lasting impression of the track is one of light-hearted holiday cheer shared between friends.

## 'BABY COME ROUND'
Duration: 3:22
Written by Spice Girls, Andy Watkins & Paul Wilson
Produced by Absolute
Mixed by Absolute
Released as a B-side with 'Who Do You Think You Are' and 'Mama' on 3 March 1997

While 'Baby Come Round' was left off the band's debut album, it showcases a band hunting for their winning formula. The latter half features an attitude-packed rap from Mel B, a device that was later employed in several other *Spice* tracks to give the Spice Girls an edge that middling pop acts of the era were missing. Otherwise, the song belongs to Mel C, whose vocal proficiency guides the ship. With both Melanies in high gear, the Spice Girls make a compelling case for why listeners should come around to their way of lovin'.

## 'FEED YOUR LOVE'
Duration: 5:13
Written by Spice Girls, Matt Rowe & Richard Stannard
Produced by Matt Rowe & Richard Stannard
Engineered by Adrian Bushby
Released on the *Wannabe 25* commemorative EP on 27 August 2021

This sultry ballad from the 1995 *Spice* sessions with Matt and Biff sat in the vault for a quarter century before seeing a formal release. It was written during the Spice Girls' inaugural trip to Strongroom Studios to work with Matt and Biff. 'The very first song we all wrote together was called "Feed Your Love",' Mel C confirmed in her memoir *The Sporty One*. After dedicating a few days to shaping the song, it was abandoned so that the group could focus their efforts elsewhere, on a little number called 'Wannabe'. While it didn't make the cut for their debut album, the time they spent crafting it wasn't in vain. A demo of the track would soon help capture the attention of Andy Watkins and Paul Wilson at Absolute, a team that would be essential to the development of *Spice*. 'They played us a few tracks [of their own] which we didn't particularly like,' Andy Watkins revealed. 'But they played us a lot of other stuff that was actually rather dark and cool, particularly a track called "Feed Your Love". So we thought, "This is OK. We can work with this."'

'I get a rush when I look at you, there's a burning inside of me,' Mel B purrs at the song's onset. In a rare move for the spotlight-sharing girl group, Mel B's four bandmates fade into background roles while she undeniably takes the lead, her vocals brimming with sensuous longing. The pulsing beat is steady and seductive. 'Feed your love to me', the Spice Girls plead in the chorus, 'cause I need to know that you care'. The song was mainly scrapped for one reason. '[It] was a bit too... raunchy,' Mel C explained. '[It] was a kind of downtempo, quite erotic song,' Biff concurred. 'It was feed your love as in giving a blow job. It was a great song, but too rude and probably a bit downtempo for the first album. Even now, it's one of my favourite records that they've ever done.'

The band was cognisant that the sexual undertones could alienate the younger demographic and with the goal of achieving wider appeal the track was shelved, a forward-thinking move given how much of their eventual success was owed to their passionate fanbase of children.

In 2016, a small fragment of the song was leaked online and in 2021 'Feed Your Love' was officially released to commemorate the 25th anniversary of 'Wannabe'.

## 'STEP TO ME'

Duration: 4:05
Written by Spice Girls and Eliot Kennedy
Produced by Absolute
Mixed by Absolute
Released as a Pepsi exclusive on 28 July 1997

'Step to Me' is an attitude-heavy track in which the Spice Girls challenge a dishonest partner head-on. The rock-influenced confrontation features Mel C inviting a suitor to wake up and smell the coffee and Mel B issuing a reminder to 'Check yourself if you think I'm gonna stand for that'.

In July 1997, the first of 92 million spiced up Pepsi products hit shelves in conjunction with the Spice Girls' lucrative partnership with the brand. The promotional cans had vibrant fuchsia pull tabs instead of the typical silver and were emblazoned with pink images of the band taken by Francesca Sorrenti in August 1996. After collecting 20 pink pull tabs, buyers could mail them into Pepsi (along with a cheque for £0.50 to cover the cost of postage) to receive a jewel case CD featuring the exclusive 7' single and three remixes. 'Hi people!!' read the text on the printed booklet therein, typed in a white font resembling hand scrawled cursive. 'We feel really delighted and proud to be able to give something back to you, the real fans who have supported us so much, so please accept our CD dedicated especially to you, it's absolutely free and exclusive to this release in the summer of 1997.' Calling it free was slightly generous given how many Pepsi products needed to be purchased to get a copy of the coveted disc but the sentiment landed. Those who sent away for their copy of 'Step to Me' were also automatically entered into a draw to win tickets to see the band's live concert debut in Istanbul, Turkey, a location selected because of Pepsi's dominance in that market.

Due to the timing of the Pepsi campaign, 'Step to Me' bridged the gap between the release of *Spice* and *Spiceworld* and was the last contribution from co-writer Eliot Kennedy until the Spice Girls' third album, *Forever*. His absence from *Spiceworld* was his own personal decision—frantically writing and recording an album with the band on a tight schedule sounded like a terrible experience. 'When I heard from Absolute and Matt and Biff how it was going and what a nightmare it was turning into, I thought, 'I don't want to get involved,' Eliot explained. 'This is not what I'm into.' Instead, 'Step to Me' was rescued from the bin from their *Spice* sessions together. Thematically it fits in with the subject matter of *Spice*; before the complications of fame and fortune became fodder for future material, they were more relatably complaining about bad boyfriends.

For the majority of Spice Girls fans, the track was available exclusively through Pepsi sweepstakes, something that ruffled the feathers of retailers who felt jilted by a promotion that circumvented record shops to distribute new music, especially after they supported the girl group when they were unknowns. Only fans in Japan were spared the extra legwork of collecting tabs, as the song was automatically included on *Spiceworld* as a bonus track when it was released on 1 November 1997, sandwiched between 'Move Over' and 'Do It' sequentially. On this version, Mel B's signature rap section uses a different vocal performance, a take in which Mel is more laid back on the beat and gentler with her diction. The song received a wide release for the first time in 2022 when it was included on a 25th anniversary edition of *Spiceworld*.

An estimated 600,000 CDs were redeemed by fans, a robust number that is, apparently, still growing. In 2023, Euan Robertson of Edinburgh, Scotland discovered some collectible pink tabs stashed in an old Lego container that he'd collected but then abandoned when he was a teen. On a whim he sent them off to Pepsi and surprisingly found a 'Step to Me' CD in his post box a few weeks later. The promotion helped pull in some new fans a full 26 years after the original campaign had concluded. 'We've since been having a Spice Girls binge on Spotify,' Euan told *Yahoo News*. 'My daughter is loving it—we're keeping girl power alive in 2023.'

# 3
## *Spiceworld*

The Spice Girls' second album, *Spiceworld,* was released in the UK on 4 November 1997 and debuted at No. 1. It remains the fastest-selling album by a girl group of all time. It was the fourth best-selling album of 1997 in the UK, coming in right behind *Spice* which was still flying off shelves. The album spent three weeks at No. 1 and yielded four singles, three of which topped the charts. *Spiceworld* was certified double platinum in over a dozen countries and to date it has sold over 20 million copies worldwide.

### 'Spice Up Your Life'
Duration: 2:53
Written by Spice Girls, Matt Rowe & Richard Stannard
Produced by Matt Rowe & Richard Stannard
Recorded and engineered by Adrian Bushby
Mixed by Mark 'Spike' Stent
Assisted by Paul 'P.Dub' Walton
Keyboards and programming by Matt Rowe
Additional programming by Pete Davis
Additional engineering by Jake Davies
Single released 13 October 1997

By the spring of 1997, Spicemania had reached a fever pitch. The band was everywhere and seemed to be involved in everything—in the span of a single month they released their first book, *Girl Power!*, which sold 200,000 copies in the first day prompting translations in over

20 languages; they made their American television debut as the musical guest on Saturday Night Live in front of an audience of 20 million home viewers; they helped launch Channel 5 in the UK with a colourful ad campaign; and they completed a promotional tour of East Asia. Instead of taking a break, they chose to capitalise on the moment and on 10 May 1997, they staged a theatrical entrance to the prestigious Cannes Film Festival via speedboat to make an announcement: a Spice Girls feature film and their sophomore album would both be released before the end of the year. The only wrinkle in this otherwise exciting plan was that neither the album nor the film had begun production, meaning that to meet this aggressive timeline both projects would need to be completed simultaneously over one busy summer.

Inspired heavily by The Beatles and their film *A Hard Day's Night*, the Spice Girls had always hoped to make the leap to the silver screen and in early 1997 they thought their opportunity had come when Disney presented the band a completed script and offered them a film deal. Part of the appeal of the Spice Girls, however, was that they were candid and perhaps a little rough around the edges so the band and manager Simon were left unimpressed by Disney's hokey concept. They passed. At that point Simon's older brother, television writer Kim Fuller, asked if he could take a shot at developing a script that better captured the band's essence. He wrote a rough draft of the film with the working title *Five* and did his best to ensure it gelled with the group's sensibilities. 'I talked to them and hung out with them a bit to get a sense of their characters and who they were,' Kim told *Vice* in 2018. 'I thought, "You can't expect the girls to act characters, so let's just let them be themselves. I'll make it a week in their life and make it surreal and kind of weird."' The film follows the Spice Girls in the days leading up to their big concert at Royal Albert Hall but the narrative is anything but linear. The group slips into different scenarios spanning countless genres, bringing to life the pitches of a pair of Hollywood screenwriters played by Mark McKinney and George Wendt, just two of many celebrity cameos. 'The film got bigger and bigger and everyone wanted to be in it,' Kim continued. Ginger Spice transforms into Bob Hoskins in one scene, then Richard O'Brien from *The Rocky Horror Picture Show* climbs out of a toilet in the next, then the Spice Girls are in court with judge Stephen Fry. A steady stream of familiar faces star in a series of vignettes, each more outlandish than the last, making the finished product feel like a bizarre fever dream. Directed by the BAFTA award-winning Bob Spiers, known for his work on the acclaimed television comedies *Fawlty Towers* and *Absolutely Fabulous*, the film had a relatively modest budget of £4 million. With Twickenham

Studios as a homebase, (and 40 other filming locations around London to ensure the film was as distinctly British as the film's lead actresses) *Spice World The Movie* was shot in just 43 days between June to August of 1997, a compressed timeline even before factoring in that an album needed to be written and recorded within the same window.

During any available breaks and at the end of long filming days, the exhausted Spice Girls would drag themselves into one of many studio spaces at their disposal to try and write new music. Writers Matt Rowe and Biff Stannard were back after their chart-topping contributions to *Spice* however their second round with the girl group would test their patience. 'I remember when they came in to record "Spice Up Your Life". It was in the middle of the chaos,' Matt vented in *Wannabe: How The Spice Girls Reinvented Pop*. To ensure everything on their ever-expanding to-do list got done, the band sometimes got a little creative and did multiple jobs at once. After waiting all day for the band to show up in studio, Matt and Biff were beyond exasperated to find that they were rolling in with an MTV film crew in tow. 'I think we only had half an hour that day too,' Mel C recalled guiltily, seeing in hindsight how difficult the situation was for their collaborators. Matt and Biff were irate. 'Well, how on earth can you possibly do this?' Matt exploded. 'You can't write and record a song in half an hour with a film crew watching. People in offices all round Whitfield Street were bombarding them—throwing things through the window, getting into the building, phoning up all the time. There [were] big crowds in the street outside.' Wherever the Spice Girls went, a circus followed.

'Eventually we got rid of the film crew and the song was done in one afternoon,' Matt said. 'All the writing and the recording of their vocals as well.' Inspiration for the track first struck during a promotional trip to Acapulco, Mexico in May 1997 when the Spice Girls fell in love with the lively Latin music that followed them wherever they went. They vowed to channel this flair into a song of their own and the result of that pledge is 'Spice Up Your Life', a riotous romp with a samba rhythm and a party spirit. Biff shared that it was conceived as an international rallying cry. 'We were talking about Bollywood films, the colours and how the Spice Girls could present themselves,' Biff shared. 'It was a matter of how do we get everything into one song?' They first set the drums in place and with a tribal rhythm established the rest fell into place. Mel B compared the ease and electricity of the writing session to what they experienced two years earlier while creating 'Wannabe' and since their tight schedule didn't allow for even a moment of writer's block these fast and effective sessions were a blessing. 'It was mayhem. Instead of taking turns to go into the vocal booths we sang the chorus all together,' Mel B wrote in her memoir *Catch A Fire*. 'That's why the final mix sounds so spontaneous and full of energy.' The track took longer to mix than it did to write and record because the wild recording environment required some additional smoothing. The track was completed just one day before it was needed for the big closing scene in *Spice World The Movie*—Simon Fuller had promised the film crew that it would be ready on time and a dedicated team of writers and producers overextended themselves in the studio to make his promise true.

'Spice Up Your Life' celebrates the 'colours of the world', a declaration that fit in seamlessly with their pre-existing message of acceptance and individuality. While this can be explained away as nothing more than a masterful branding move to rope in fans of all origins, a message of inclusion was always important to the Spice Girls. As a mixed-race woman who experienced intolerance and harassment firsthand as far back as she could remember, this was paramount for Mel B. She was born and raised in Leeds by her white, English mother, Andrea Dixon, and her black father, Martin Wingrove Brown, who spent his early years on the Caribbean island of Nevis and moved to England with his parents as a nine-year-old boy. He was one of the only black people in the predominantly white area of Chapeltown, something he was never able to forget due to a constant barrage of racist comments and concerted community ostracisation. 'When I was a baby and my parents were in town, Mum would make Dad carry me because it was less likely he'd be attacked if he had a baby in his arms,' Mel wrote in a 2021 piece for *The Sun*. Some of her earliest memories are of otherisation. 'I was aware from a very young age that I didn't see many other people of my colour... it was really when I went to school that I understood the colour of my skin had such an effect on the other kids. I used to get chased home by kids shouting these names at me, so I learnt to run fast.' She drew the ire of black people and white people alike, accepted by neither because they all viewed her as an outsider. 'I was called half-breed, half-caste and redskin, which were terms I really hated,' she said.

Before auditions for their new girl group kicked off, Heart Management already knew they wanted to fill one of the positions with a black woman—a diverse lineup would jumpstart their cross-demographic appeal. Knowledge of this prerequisite weighed on Mel and she was left questioning the legitimacy of her talent and competence. 'I'd like to think that I was chosen to be in the group on the strength of my personality, rather than as the token black girl. I still don't know to this day,' Mel reflected in her 2002 memoir. While it was apparent to others that Mel possessed many traits that made her invaluable to the girl group, she herself couldn't distinguish where her merits ended and where her quota-satisfying qualities began. Her singularity in the industry was painfully apparent to her. 'There were never any black people at the meetings we went to as Spice Girls,' she said. 'Not one black face in all those high-up meetings with the heads of this company and that company and their marketing managers and financial directors. It really bothered me.' When she pointed it out to the other four girls, they stressed that they didn't see her colour, only the content of her character. She understood that they were trying to help but these comments made it clear they just couldn't relate to what she was experiencing.

Even when the Spice Girls became one of the biggest musical acts in the world it wasn't enough to protect Mel B from discrimination. Bigotry hung over important career milestones like an insidious cloud, tainting achievements that should have been reason to celebrate. In November 1997, the Spice Girls visited South Africa to meet president and anti-apartheid activist Nelson Mandela, an enormous honour for the girl group who understood his legacy as a champion of human rights. During some down time, the Spice Girls took a trip into Sun City to go shopping. As they browsed in a designer clothing store an agitated sales assistant beelined for Mel B and asked her to leave. The other four girls were appalled. 'Of course, all the girls had a go at the assistant because they were so shocked,' Mel remembered. 'It's pretty awful to think I wasn't actually shocked because if you are brown then there's always a part of you that expects some confrontation.' Just a few weeks later, they would be subjected to another boldfaced racial ambush when the band appeared on the Dutch TV program *Laat de Leeu*. Mid-conversation presenter Paul De Leeuw abruptly introduced Santa Claus' helper Zwarte Piet, or Black Pete, and five actors emerged on stage in full blackface, sporting afro wigs, gold hoop earrings, and large red painted lips, playing offensive caricatures straight from a nineteenth-century minstrel show. The Spice Girls were visibly uncomfortable and immediately objected to the racist display. Mel B spoke up. 'I think they shouldn't paint their faces. You should get proper black people to do it,' she said firmly. 'I don't think that's very good.' The host downplayed the issue, justifying it as part of Danish culture to which the Spice Girls made a polite recommendation: 'Update your culture.'

Mel B felt compelled to use her platform as a Spice Girl to represent young black and mixed-race girls. Growing up, she saw how people of colour were excluded from mainstream storytelling, either appearing as tired old stereotypes or not appearing at all. Popular media shapes the way people see the world and a lack of representation renders entire communities as invisible. Mel was conscious of the power that came with visibility, and she wanted young girls to be able to turn on MTV and see someone who looked like them not just being tolerated but being celebrated. When the styling team from Virgin recommended that Mel straighten her hair for the 'Wannabe' music video she pushed back without hesitation. 'I refused point-blank because my hair was my identity and yes it was different to all the other girls but that was what the Spice Girls were about—celebrating our differences,' she reflected later. 'I wanted my fro to be out there as a symbol of who I was, my Yorkshire accent to speak for me and my attitude always to be proud of my identity,' Mel said in 2023. Her determination to be visibly and proudly mixed-race carried a lot of significance—she received letters from emotional mothers expressing gratitude that their daughters had someone to 'be' when dancing with classmates. Suddenly, they were proud to wear their hair naturally, to be themselves. These stories moved Mel and reinforced that she was making a difference. Her mere existence was empowering all the colours of the world.

When filming wrapped on *Spice World The Movie,* the Spice Girls had to immediately shift their focus to their upcoming album, *Spiceworld,* for which 'Spice Up Your Life' was selected as the lead single. The band travelled to New York City to shoot the music video with German director Marcus Nispel on 6 and 7 September 1997. 'I think there are very few artists who are willing to do fun stuff right now [...] so I always enjoy if somebody comes along that's a bit more theatrical,' Marcus said about his desire to work with the band. Inspired by Ridley Scott's 1982 science fiction film *Blade Runner,* the video takes place in a dark and futuristic cityscape that's now ruled by the formidable girl group. In this world, television stations only broadcast Spice Girls-related content and all corporations have been replaced with spiced-up equivalents. The five-piece, styled in dark outfits and heavy makeup, surveys their new kingdom from an aircraft before emerging from the vessel on hoverboards to weave between skyscrapers and billboards bearing their images. 'Strangely we weren't consulted about how it should look, as we normally were,' Mel B wrote in her memoir. 'We'd discussed it among ourselves and definitely saw it as one long carnival party scene, but that's not what we got.' The dark backdrop of the city reads as somewhat sinister, a world away from the colourful Bollywood-inspired spectacle that the girls envisioned during the writing process. 'We didn't have the time (or energy) to argue, though,' Mel B continued. 'I guess the end result linked into the theme of world domination, but it wasn't right.

I don't think any of us liked it much, even though we enjoyed making it. I still can't understand what's going on in it half the time.'

Once again pulling double-duty, the Spice Girls provided a peek behind the scenes in a segment with Andi Peters for ITV's *The Noise*. 'I'm the Statue of Liberty! You know, with a twist,' Geri told him on the video set. She wore a black version of the monument's spiked diadem and crafted her own torch by scrounging up a lightbulb and affixing it to a hook—'Spice Up Your Life' was the most expensive music video in the band's history but even as the Spice Girls' budget grew, Geri was unable to shed her DIY roots. She explained her handcrafted prop to ITV's camera, visibly proud of her creation. While the atmosphere on set was upbeat, privately it was an emotional day for the group. Just a week earlier, the world was shocked by the tragic death of Princess Diana and the first day of the 'Spice Up Your Life' shoot coincided with the funeral. Two billion people tuned in across the globe to watch the televised service and the Spice Girls were no exception. 'I tried not to cry. I failed miserably,' Geri revealed in her memoir *If Only*. 'I sat in a limousine, watching the funeral on the small screen. It was early in the morning in New York and I had just spent an hour having my makeup done at the hotel. I wore a thick black mask of eye shadow to cover my sad face. The make-up was leaking down my cheeks.'

The Spice Girls respectfully delayed the release of 'Spice Up Your Life' in honour of Princess Diana and her grieving family. The band was undoubtedly affected by the tragedy but this was also likely a business decision—Elton John's tribute to the late princess, 'Candle in the Wind' was breaking sales records and remained at No. 1 for five weeks which would have blocked the Spice Girls from their goal. When 'Spice Up Your Life' was finally released on 13 October 1997, the song was a more moderate success and received less radio play internationally than preceding singles. 'The laws of physics hold that for every action there is an equal and opposite reaction, so it should come as no surprise that the global success of the Spice Girls has spawned a nasty backlash,' began one 1997 *MTV* article on the Spice exhaustion that many were starting to experience. The article went on to promote an online Whack-A-Mole game for those who'd 'had it up to here with the perpetually sassy British pop outfit' that allowed users to smack the Spice Girls back into their holes. As hostile sentiments towards the group swelled publicly, breakup rumours began to circulate. The group adamantly denied them.

Despite some backlash, 'Spice Up Your Life' was still a major commercial success. It debuted at No. 1 in the UK, selling 321,000 copies in the first week. It was the tenth biggest single of the year and the band's fifth consecutive song to top the charts.

## 'STOP'

Duration: 3:24
Written by Spice Girls, Andy Watkins & Paul Wilson
Produced by Absolute
Engineered by Jeremy Wheatley
Mixed by Mark 'Spike' Stent
Assisted by Paul 'P.Dub' Walton
Additional programming by Mike Higham
Brass by Kick Horns
Guitar by Milton McDonald
All other instruments by Absolute
Released as a single 9 March 1998

Upon learning that the Spice Girls' sophomore album needed to be written in tandem with the filming of a major motion picture, Absolute's Andy Watkins and Paul Wilson were immediately concerned. Forcing a burned-out band to think creatively on a tight schedule sounded like a recipe for disaster but the producers were assured that a mobile recording studio would be erected on set, giving the Spice Girls an easily accessible space to workshop new material between scenes. This reassurance, combined with Absolute's earnest desire to work with the group again, sold them on the idea, however they quickly learned that their hesitation was justified. 'We'd sit there literally all day long and quite often we wouldn't even get them at all,' Andy said of the on-set studio, a concept that worked much better in theory than in practice. The seeds of 'Stop' were sewn in this hectic environment in something Mel C referred to as a 'drive-by session'.

While drifting to sleep one night, the first few lines of a new song popped into Geri's head. She bolted out of bed and crooned the snippets into a Dictaphone to ensure the fragments weren't forgotten and when she arrived on set the next morning, she tore into the mobile studio to bark at Andy and Paul. 'I had an idea: stop right there! Thank you very much—right, gotta go.' With that the door of the trailer slammed shut and Geri was gone, running to set to begin another lengthy day of filming. While not an ideal way to collaborate, this at least gave Absolute a springboard. 'Because we were so desperate to write with them, we were literally holding on to any kind of input that they were giving us,'

Paul explained in *Wannabe: How The Spice Girls Reinvented Pop*. Using Geri's scraps, the team built a melody line and assembled a backing track. Andy and Paul were eventually able to steal some time with the girls to further develop the track. 'Mel C [...] finished off the chorus and, later, when we had more time, the other girls came in and helped write the verses and bridge,' Geri recalled. The song had a Motown swagger with a thumping drumbeat and punchy horns reminiscent of The Supremes; the Spice Girls could already visualize a music video featuring synchronised Motown-style choreography and 1960s fashions to complement the song's retro sound. Even with creative constraints and limited time, the Spice Girls were able to infuse a track with personality. 'Between us, whether we wrote just a bit of the song or a lot of it, we added that Spice Girls magic,' Mel C concluded in *The Sporty One*.

'It was with Paul and Andy that I became the resident Spice Girl ad-libber,' Mel C said of her signature contribution to the Spice Girls songbook. 'It's quite a technical thing, but I'll try my best to explain it... Just sing any old shit!' she joked in her 2022 memoir. Mel's powerful voice frequently heightened the stakes during a track's conclusion, something she achieved by improvising vocal riffs over the chorus. 'You bounce around the melody adding new ideas, breaths, 'oohs' 'ahhs' and high bits,' she elaborated. 'It's so spontaneous and creative. You have to lose your self-consciousness and go for it [...] but if you feel free, you never know when the magic is going to happen.' This tactic, when paired with her dynamic vocal abilities, ensured that Spice Girls' tracks always went out with a bang, not a whimper. 'Stop' features this technique prominently and when she wails the song's final lyrics with zeal her parting gift is one final adrenaline boost. 'Thank you very much, thank you very much!'

At its core, 'Stop' is a snapshot of the band's emotional state in the summer of 1997. Although only a year had elapsed since they were catapulted to fame with the release of 'Wannabe', it had been an unrelenting year and the Spice Girls were running out of steam. They knew that the pace established by manager Simon Fuller was unsustainable. 'That song was about how we were feeling about Simon, about how hard we were working and how much was going on,' Mel C reflected. 'We just needed to stop, we just needed to catch our breath. We just needed to slow down.' Simon understood that the public's Spice obsession couldn't last forever so he was eager to squeeze every opportunity, and dollar, out of it while he could. That meant cramming as much as possible into every single day—interviews, photoshoots, brand deals, new music, a movie. The to-do list seemed endless.

In *Spice World The Movie*, the band's manager Clifford, portrayed by actor Richard E. Grant, is a not-so-subtle allusion to Simon. During a climactic scene in which the band fights for a modicum of independence, an enraged Clifford seethes, 'You don't have a life, you have a schedule!' This was the reality of life for the Spice Girls. 'We'd had this huge, massive success with our first album and, rather than celebrate that and take time to recuperate and plan the next stage of our career, we went straight into the second album, with a film dumped on top for good measure,' Mel C reflected in her memoir. 'It was non-stop and I think a wiser person might have put in a break at this point.' Simon earned a 20 per cent cut of the Spice Girls' earnings, more than any individual Spice Girl made, so he was highly incentivised to keep the band working. While Simon wanted to earn as much as possible, the band just wanted time to catch their breath, something they transparently address in the bridge of 'Stop': 'I don't care about the money, don't be wasting my time / You need less speed, get off my case / You gotta slow it down baby, just get out of my face.'

The band's dissatisfaction with Simon extended beyond scheduling to include his management style which allegedly relied heavily on psychological manipulation. In her 2002 memoir, Mel B accused Simon of playing emotional games to keep the band in check. 'If you were to note down how Simon operated with us, it was very, very clever, very precise and very planned,' Mel B said. 'The emotional waves the band went through were very much down to him.' If he was displeased with one of the girls, he wouldn't directly confront them but would instead stir up conflict by making subtle comments to her bandmates. 'While we weren't entirely impenetrable before Simon came along, after his arrival the cracks between us started to widen,' Mel C noticed. When he was away, things ran smoothly but as soon as he returned the girls were once again at one another's throats. 'It took us ages to work out what was going on because for a long time we were moving far too fast to notice,' Mel B corroborated. He played favourites but the object of his affection would shift on a dime, leaving the girls confused about what they did wrong. 'Simon Fuller had always said a man will ruin this group—meaning one of our boyfriends from the outside,' Victoria wrote in her memoir *Learning To Fly*. 'But the man who started to tear the Spice Girls away from each other was him.'

The girls slogged through their overpacked summer schedule but by October 1997 the pressure had become unbearable. Geri, who'd struggled with disordered eating for most of her adult life, was battling bulimia. She approached Simon to explain that she needed a week off to receive professional treatment. Simon listened to Geri's tearful plea before shaking his head. The answer was no. 'There are two reasons, Geri,' he allegedly began according to Geri's memoir. 'One, it sets a bad precedent amongst the girls. If you take a week off, then everybody will be asking for one. And two, we sold eighteen million copies of the first album. That set the benchmark. We want to sell nineteen million copies this time.' His coldness rattled Geri and she realised that he was no longer acting in the best interest of her and her bandmates. While there had been whispers of dissatisfaction between the girls in the preceding months, it was this incident that prompted Geri to contact the Spice Girls' lawyer to explore their legal options.

Simon Fuller was fired on 6 November 1997 while the Spice Girls were in Rotterdam, Netherlands for the MTV Europe Awards. As the band climbed on stage to accept the award for Best Group, Simon was back in New York City learning of his dismissal from the band's legal representation. 'The Spice Girls are hugely grateful to 19 Management but we feel in our hearts that this is the right decision for us,' they said in an official statement. The tabloids had taken to calling Simon 'Svengali Spice' and painted him as the puppet master responsible for the band's every success (conveniently ignoring that the girls had written most of *Spice* before even meeting him). With Simon out of the picture the press gleefully predicted the impending downfall of the Spice Girls. But while in the eye of the media storm, the girls just forged ahead and focused on promoting *Spiceworld*. 'In the same way as we'd done with [Heart Management] three years before, we were taking our career into our own hands,' Mel C said.

On 27 January 1998, the Spice Girls descended onto Carnew Street, a residential pocket in Dublin's Stoneybatter neighbourhood, to film the music video for 'Stop'. The band had been rehearsing for their imminent world tour in nearby County Kildare but proximity was not the only benefit of filming in Stoneybatter; the rowhouse-lined streets conjured visions of working-class Britain circa 1960, perfect for the retro atmosphere that the Spice Girls were chasing. In wardrobes consisting of pleated miniskirts, tailored pantsuits, go-go boots, and fabulous overcoats, the Spice Girls looked like they had time travelled back to the Swinging Sixties.

In Stoneybatter, the day of the 'Stop' video shoot remains a modern legend that's been woven into the fabric of the neighbourhood. The unannounced arrival of the world's biggest girl group rocked the small community and residents still boast about their brushes with the popstars to this day. 'Emma Bunton went into Mrs. O'Brien's house up the road,' one resident spilled excitedly in a 2019 *IrishCentral* retrospective. Another resident bragged about getting a hug from Ginger Spice during a lunch break. Seemingly everyone in the neighbourhood (or their grandmother, or their cousin's friend) had a story to share about their encounter with the Spice Girls. 'It's against the law to walk up Carnew Street and not mention the Spice Girls,' joked one resident. 'It's definitely a matter of pride for the area.' Residents signed contracts agreeing not to photograph or film the girls while the production was in progress and were each paid £100 to compensate for the inconvenience of the shoot, however, most seemed thrilled by the intrusion. In this pre-smartphone era, news of the celebrity visitors briefly remained a local secret. Within the neighbourhood, however, the gossip spread quickly and by midday children were skipping school to visit Carnew Street in the hopes that they'd catch a glimpse of the larger-than-life popstars. Video producers had combed the area in advance and selected extras to appear in the video; however, the musical act was not identified until the day of the shoot. 'The casting call was shrouded in secrecy, and I assumed I was auditioning to be in a Carter Twins or some other Irish pop acts' video,' said Marian Noble, who appeared in the video as a young girl. 'Never in a million years did I imagine it was for the Spice Girls.'

Directed by James Brown, the 'Stop' video is brimming with an organic playfulness. 'It wasn't planned down to the last detail and was quite a free-for-all,' Mel B said of their approach. Without storyboards or rigid outlines, the band was free to indulge in the schoolyard games of their youth. The Spice Girls emerge from their respective homes to convene in the middle of the road where they joyfully dance before playing hopscotch and cat's cradle with the local children. A beaming Mel C jumps rope, Emma plays pattycake, Victoria hula hoops, Geri rides a horse, and Mel B faces off against locals in a game of coconut shy. The latter part of the video is set in a fairground, filmed in Rathdrum village in County Wicklow the day after the Carnew Street shoot. The narrative concludes with the band on stage in a dusty town hall crooning into vintage microphones. The Spice Girls win over a crowd of surly audience members who cannot help but be swept up in their joyful performance, demonstrating that they learned the moral of the story: everyone needs to slow down and have some fun.

'Stop' was released on 9 March 1998 and was the first of the Spice Girls' seven singles to fall short of the No. 1 spot on the UK charts. Jason Nevins' remix of 'It's Like That' by Run-D.M.C. was an unexpected hit that stayed at No. 1 for six weeks, freezing the Spice Girls at No. 2.

The band took this defeat hard as they feared it gave credence to the idea that they were crumbling without Simon at the helm. Despite their disappointment, the track was well-received by critics with David Browne of *Entertainment Weekly* calling it, 'a delicious re-creation of Motown-era bop packed with skipping-down-the-street good vibrations'. As of 2024, it is one of their most streamed tracks on Spotify, surpassed only by the all-powerful 'Wannabe'.

## 'Too Much'

Duration: 4:31
Written by Spice Girls, Andy Watkins & Paul Wilson
Produced by Absolute
Engineered by Paul Hicks
Assisted by Robbie Kazandjian
Mixed by Mark 'Spike' Stent
Assisted by Jan Kybert
Additional programming by Mike Higham
Brass by Kick Horns
Guitar by Milton McDonald
Strings arranged by Stephen Hussey
Strings performed by 'Pure Stringz'
All other instruments by Absolute
Released as a single 15 December 1997

'Too Much' was written during a prosperous period of the band's history. 'Everything we touched turned to gold, it was ridiculous,' Mel C recalled in the 2012 ITV documentary *The Spice Girls Story: Viva Forever!* But with new levels of success came new problems. '"Too Much" was a really difficult time,' she continued. 'We were just… I mean, beyond exhausted.' It was an emotionally conflicting situation for the Spice Girls—all of their wildest dreams had come true and they were immensely grateful, but their workload was unmanageable and they weren't granted even a moment to recharge. 'So much is going on and it's all so brilliant and we don't want it to stop and we can't let it stop but, you know, how long can we keep this up?' Mel C said of her headspace at the time. 'It actually feels like a bit of a blur,' Emma recounted. 'Just being so tired, coming off set and walking straight onto a mobile studio. Sometimes having an hour in one studio and then an hour back on set… madness.' On top of the album and the film, the Spice Girls also had a litany of other obligations. Andy and Paul remember scouring the set in search of one Spice Girl who needed to complete her vocals for 'Too Much' only to find her sequestered in a back room reviewing clothing options for the upcoming line of Spice Girls dolls.

Because dedicated studio time was a rarity, the girls had to work on the fly and harvest ideas where they could. Everywhere she went, Geri carried with her a small red notebook in which she jotted down interesting turns of phrase or potential song concepts. When an on-set security guard asked Geri for an autograph but had nothing for her to sign she autographed his top instead—'What part of no don't you understand?' the novelty T-shirt asked in bold letters. Into the notebook it went. Another piece of 'Too Much' fell into place around the same time. 'I'd just finished [filming] for the day and I was in my car alone and couldn't get out the gates because there were so many fans outside,' she recounted. During filming of the movie, fans would show up on set in droves, an exciting experience for those who left with tales of a celebrity sighting but for Geri, who was trapped in an immovable horde, it was a little scary. 'I was sitting there thinking, "Oh my god", and I started writing some of the lyrics to the chorus.' These thoughts, as well as some scribbled ruminations about love being blind and how meaningless thoughts can be framed to sound deep, were later refined and woven together. The time constraints established a pattern for the band's *Spiceworld* material—just as with 'Stop', Geri shouted a few scattered ideas at Andy and Paul before being rushed away to other work commitments. The pair were left trying extract a song out of Geri's random flashes of inspiration, but they again managed to develop the number's musical foundation. 'We started working on it and we wanted to do some sort of doo-wop vocal thing,' Paul said. 'So we constructed this backing track and then more of the girls started to come in—this was quite a good day—and gradually they started to add on their little bits.' It was typical for the band to interject their ideas at different stages of the writing process when their schedules would allow. '[T]he songs had to be more ambiguous, with the meanings open to interpretation so that each of us could read into the lyrics what we wanted to,' Geri elaborated in her memoir.

The Spice Girls sometimes felt like they were drowning in work commitments, and 'Too Much' definitely reflects that, but for Geri the song was also about insatiability—her ever-shifting goalpost trapped her in a state of dissatisfaction, always convinced that the next achievement would be the key to her happiness and true success. 'You just want more, more, more, but it's never enough. And yet you can't let it go either,' Geri shared in *The Spice Girls Story: Viva Forever!* 'You know that hunger for something, whether it's love, whether it's money, whether it's fame.' The Spice Girls had welcomed, and even prayed for, fame when they were starting out, believing celebrity status to be the ultimate form of validation and acceptance. 'Fame for me was always like a solution for disappointment,' Geri reflected. 'When the boy didn't love me back or I didn't get the job, I thought well if I become successful and famous all of you will be sorry.' By pinning so much of her self-worth on fame, she was setting herself up for failure. She learned that there was no magic button that could be pressed to instantaneously solve all her issues. In many ways, being in the spotlight heightened the Spice Girls' insecurities. Hateful comments cut deeper than ever and they were mortified to see their flaws being examined under a microscope. Meanwhile, the adoration of fans set impossibly high expectations that the girls felt pressure to live up to. The Spice Girls were seen as beautiful and witty and stylish and energetic and charming—how could someone manage to be all those things all the time and, an even more anxiety-inducing thought, what would happen if they faltered?

Two weeks after writing 'Too Much' the Spice Girls recorded the track between takes for the movie—that day they were filming an action-packed scene on the River Thames and the public spectacle drew a large crowd. 'The fans had found out where we were and mobbed the set,' Mel C remembered. 'One by one we'd be hustled in to see Andy and Paul to try and get our vocals down but there was pandemonium going on outside.' Paul remembered the chaos as well. 'Security had left for the day and it turned into a bit of a riot,' he reminisced. 'Mel B recorded the opening verse to 'Too Much' with fans rocking the van back and forth and police horses circling.' Despite the ruckus outside during the recording process, the finished product was a tranquil and mesmeric doo-wop inspired ballad. Mel C showcased her vocal capabilities at the track's climax, powerfully crooning, 'I want a man, not a boy who thinks he can.' The hypnotic repetition of the outro traps the listener in a cycle of despondence mirroring the mental state of the group at this time. In her distinctly resonant tone, Mel B spends the final minute of the track singing the jaded refrain, 'Too much of nothing so why don't we give it a try, too much of something we're gonna be living a lie', on loop over an orchestral bed.

As soon as the Spice Girls finished writing a new song, it was quickly incorporated into the movie. 'After writing 'Too Much' last week when we were in the Docklands, we decided we should have it as the opening song in the movie,' the band wrote in a diary entry for *Spice World: The Official Book of the Movie* dated Monday, 7 July 1997. 'This was only decided two days ago, so this morning we're in our winnie working out our choreography. Talk about last minute!!!' The track plays during the psychedelic opening credit sequence of the film before segueing into a live performance recorded at the Top of the Pops studio in London. Kim Fuller, the film's screenwriter, said the decision to start the film with 'Too Much' was done to bookend the film with the band's strongest new tracks, with 'Spice Up Your Life' later closing the picture. 'I loved the day we did the *TOTP* scene and sang 'Too Much,'' Mel C shared in her own diary entry. 'I think that it's my favourite song on the album, actually.'

'Too Much' was chosen as *Spiceworld*'s second single and a music video shoot was scheduled for 10 November 1997. The music video's director, Howard Greenhalgh, had been working closely with Simon on the tone and narrative of the video but by the time the shoot rolled around circumstances had changed—Simon had been fired just four days earlier. 'During the day, I felt under enormous pressure because so many negative things were being written and said about us,' Geri later wrote of the 'Too Much' shoot. The group was aware of the media backlash occurring following Simon's departure. 'The press continued to speculate about our future,' Mel B added. 'No one, it seemed, could believe that we'd be able to go it alone, including our record company. Some of the people at Virgin were very nervous about this new development in Spiceworld.' The shoot with Howard, however, went ahead as planned. 'The greatest irony about sacking Simon was that it had been triggered by my not being given a week off. Yet since then, we have worked twice as hard to prove that we didn't need him,' Geri wrote of the gruelling schedule they maintained through the end of 1997 and into 1998 as the band took over management responsibilities themselves.

The 'Too Much' video is packed with allusions to the silver screen and inserts each Spice Girl into a famous film. Mel B is dressed in dystopian chic battle-wear and sings the song's opening lines atop an armoured tank as explosions detonate behind her in a setting inspired by the 1980's Australian action film *Mad Max*. Styled in a white nightgown, Emma's segments are set in a bedroom where paranormal gusts whip the room's contents around like a scene from *Poltergeist*. Mel C is in Chinatown wearing a bold red cheongsam in an homage to *Year of the Dragon*; she delivers her lines undisturbed by the men performing elaborate fight choreography nearby. Geri's segments are filmed in black and white and her fitted white evening gown and elbow-length gloves are reminiscent of Rita Hayworth in the 1946 film *Gilda*. She sways and poses on stage with sailors acting as her backup dancers. And finally, Victoria transforms into Catwoman from *Batman Returns* by slipping into a sleek PVC bodysuit and matching cat ears while a team of rocket scientists bustle around her.

'The rushes looked great, but the day proved to be horrendously long. Poor Mel B didn't finish until 5 a.m. and was outside wearing very little,' Geri remembered of the single-day shoot. Two versions of the music video were produced, the first exclusively featuring footage from the video shoot, while the second, acting as promotional material for *Spice World The Movie*, including footage from the film.

'Too Much' was released on 15 December 1997 and debuted at the top of the charts becoming the band's sixth consecutive single to reach No. 1 in the UK. 'The Spice Girls had become the first band in thirty-two years to have two Christmas number-one singles in a row,' Geri proudly recalled in her memoir. Not since The Beatles' winning streak from 1963 to 1965 had another act achieved consecutive Christmas No. 1s. This history-making accomplishment temporarily silenced detractors who had been eagerly anticipating the band's demise following their recent management shake-up. 'The Spice Girls are incredibly popular and the cynicism of the media has not dented that,' BBC Radio 1 DJ Mark Goodier said about their triumph. 'Their second album has sold eight million copies in a few weeks. It's been their year so it's only right that they should be the Christmas No. 1.' A spokesman of the William Hill gambling company said that the Spice Girls' chart victory would cost them an estimated £100,000. 'The band are 10-1 favourites for next year. We think their bubble will have burst by then,' he added, a prediction that would age very poorly.

With the success of 'Too Much' the Spice Girls ended 1997 on a high, cruising comfortably over the high bar that they set for themselves in 1996. Their holiday season tour de force also included the release of *Spice World The Movie* which grossed £2.3 million in its opening weekend making it the highest opening gross for a British production in the UK. This box office success was soon mirrored in the United States and the worldwide gross would surpass $56 million during the film's initial theatrical run. Reviews were unflattering, with film critic Roger Ebert famously giving it half a star out of five, but he was not the Spice Girls' target demographic. For every adult male wringing his hands and ranting about the film's scattered plot or vacuous stars, existed a dozen young girls who were thrilled to watch their pop idols on the big screen.

## 'SATURDAY NIGHT DIVAS'
Duration: 4:25
Written by Spice Girls, Matt Rowe & Richard Stannard
Produced by Matt Rowe & Richard Stannard
Recorded and engineered by Adrian Bushby

Mixed by Mark 'Spike' Stent
Assisted by Paul 'P.Dub' Walton
Keyboards and programming by Matt Rowe
Additional programming by Pete Davis and Magnus Fiennes
Additional engineering by Jake Davies

'You're a twisted lover, kiss and telling on a superstar, that's what you are,' Emma chides in the pre-chorus of 'Saturday Night Divas', a glittery pop-funk singalong that brings attention to one of the major drawbacks of life in the public eye. While the Spice Girls had learned to question the motives of new acquaintances who intended to leak stories to the media for payment and clout, it stung much more when the betrayal came from someone that they had once trusted. 'Emma and Victoria had both been stitched up by former boyfriends, who'd sold pictures and details of their sex lives to the tabloids,' Geri remembered in *If Only*. In April 1997, *The Star* ran the first of three instalments of 'intimate revelations' about Posh Spice as told by her first boyfriend. 'These newspapers wanted their money's worth and made sure they got it, true or false,' Victoria ranted. 'Like he said how we had had sex in a train going up to Scotland. In your dreams, mate.' But under the anger was humiliation. Whether true or not, Victoria dreaded the thought of her dad reading lurid stories about his daughter's sex life from the paper over breakfast. 'It was just horrible, like your house being burgled, only worse,' she recalled, deflated.

The tabloids didn't bother feigning journalistic integrity and were largely uninterested in the legitimacy of the stories. Their only objective was to sell as many papers as possible and the more salacious the headline, the better. 'We used to drive to secluded spots and make love in [the car],' Emma's ex-boyfriend bragged to *The Mirror* with total disregard for his former-partner's feelings. 'She was like a cat—she liked to be stroked and caressed. She is a sweet, innocent girl, but she could surprise me.' Emma's bad luck continued when a second ex-boyfriend divulged personal details to *The Mirror*. Describing himself as Emma's first boyfriend, he boasted about taking Emma's virginity when she was 16 and he was 21, peppering in colourful and crass anecdotes as he went. The betrayal of trust and invasion of privacy devastated her. 'Afterwards, Emma and I would plot our imaginary revenge, fantasising about a well-aimed drop-kick and pouring pints of beer over their heads,' Geri recalled. 'They deserved far worse.' A chaser to many of these outrageous and invasive pieces was a call to the public: 'Have you romanced a Spice Girl? Call our hotline!' All five girls were eventually double-crossed by ex-partners but they sometimes inadvertently revealed their own shortcomings in the process—Emma's ex-boyfriend admitted that he ended the relationship because he was insecure about dating a powerful and successful woman. 'It was weird kissing a woman who was the object of a million male fantasies,' he whined. 'Everywhere we went, she was lusted after.'

The Spice Girls only performed 'Saturday Night Divas' live twice, on 12 and 13 October 1997 in their two-night Pepsi-sponsored concert debut in Istanbul, Turkey.

## 'NEVER GIVE UP ON THE GOOD TIMES'
Duration: 4:30
Written by Spice Girls, Matt Rowe & Richard Stannard
Produced by Richard Stannard & Matt Rowe
Mixed by Mark 'Spike' Stent
Assisted by Paul 'P.Dub' Walton
Keyboards and programming by Pete Davis and Magnus Fiennes
Additional engineering by Jake Davies
Bass guitar by Steve Lewison
Guitar by Shawn Lee
Flute by Snake Davis
Strings arranged by Anne Dudley

'Never Give Up on the Good Times' is an infectiously optimistic disco anthem that urges listeners to shrug off their worries and focus on the happiness that the future holds. The track is a danceable ode to the power of positive thinking and posits that when 'living it up is a state of mind' a person's joy is merely an attitude adjustment away. This was a personal philosophy of co-writer Biff Stannard who used music as a way to improve his own mood. 'I've always written myself happy, I've always written to cheer myself up,' Biff said of his songwriting approach on the *Music Business Worldwide* podcast.

The Spice Girls formed during a period where a lot of popular music lacked levity. The late 1980s and early 1990s were defined in large part by the rise of grunge, as Seattle-based bands like Nirvana, Pearl Jam, Soundgarden, and Alice in Chains rose to prominence with thick, distortion-heavy songs featuring disillusioned lyrics with scathing self-reflection that sometimes bordered on self-disgust. This rejuvenated interest in alternative rock and helped propel already established bands like The Smashing Pumpkins to new heights of mainstream success.

At the same time the industrial music scene was thriving with acts like Nine Inch Nails, Ministry, and Marilyn Manson serving up harsh tracks with dissonant soundscapes. Dr. Dre, Jay Z and Snoop Dog rose to the top of a booming rap scene populated with street-hardened personas, while a surging underground scene contributed sociopolitical statements concurrently. Sir Mix-a-Lot was singing about asses, the Red Hot Chili Peppers were singing about California, and Bryan Adams was devastating listeners with ultra-sincere ballads. As the '90s progressed, Oasis, Blur, Suede and Pulp became the faces of Britpop and paired catchy melodies with slice-of-life lyricism about sex, drugs, rock and roll, and being working class English. While there were certainly successful and insightful female musicians working (and pop music was alive and well), the landscape at the time had some overarching trends: it was very male-dominated, and the men in question were quite serious about public image.

When the Spice Girls arrived on the scene, they wholeheartedly embraced femininity and frivolity. If they found themselves somewhere stuffy, they took it upon themselves to transform the space into a party. They joked, yelled, and laughed their way through their long workdays and press appearances and welcomed everyone to join in with them. 'We were having fun, that was the main thing,' Victoria said of their key to success. '[W]e had a laugh everywhere that we went and we used to make people smile. We really did. We were funny, we had good senses of humour [...] and people liked the music.'

'Never Give Up on the Good Times' opens with a synthesizer riff that is so boisterous and bouncy that it sounds as though it's squealing with glee. It is backed by a brisk beat and peppered with sound effects that mimic a croaking frog. An organ kicks in with the first taste of the number's melody line before transitioning to a sparkling string arrangement. Instead of feeling frenetic, it feels energised. Plucks of an electric guitar punctuate every line as Geri launches into the song's first verse and listeners are treated to a soaring flute solo towards the song's close. The chorus ties the number together, urging listeners to, 'Never give up on the good times, gotta believe in the love you find'. The track would be right at home in a roller disco.

The Spice Girls wrote the song with Matt and Biff at Whitfield Street studios in June 1997. With Matt seated behind the piano, the girls surrounded him and tossed around lyric ideas over some chords. While some adjustments were made to the lyrics between the jam session and the finished product (such as the lyric 'never look back on the bad times' being ditched and the main melody line undergoing a slight tuning), the general concept for the song came together quickly and remained constant. It shares musical similarities with another feel-good jam, 'Let's Groove' by Earth, Wind & Fire, and also has lyrical and musical parallels with George Benson's 'Never Give Up on a Good Thing'. The group planned to release the song as a double A-side single with 'Viva Forever' in the spring of 1998 but the idea was dropped after their release schedule was delayed and 'Viva Forever' was ultimately released on its own. Although never a single, the song is still an important piece of their catalogue that encapsulates the Spice Girls' message. When Emma was asked in a 1998 interview what one thing the Spice Girls should be remembered for after Spicemania dissipates, she did not hesitate. 'Positivity,' she said with conviction.

'MOVE OVER'
Duration: 2:46
Written by Spice Girls, Mary Wood, Clifford Lane, Richard Stannard & Matt Rowe
Produced by Richard Stannard & Matt Rowe
Recorded and engineered by Adrian Bushby
Mixed by Mark 'Spike' Stent
Assisted by Paul 'P.Dub' Walton
Keyboards and programming by Matt Rowe
Additional programming by Pete Davis
Additional engineering by Jake Davies

Prior to its release on the Spice Girls' sophomore album, 'Move Over' had already made a splash on television screens across the globe in a series of adverts for Pepsi's 'Generation Next' campaign. Filmed in Los Angeles on 19 March 1997, the ad was an energetic collage of the Spice Girls jumping around in an alleyway with Pepsi logos stamped on the palms of their hands and their signature platform shoes as 'Move Over' blared. The Spice Girls wrote the song with two new collaborators, Mary Wood and Clifford Lane of the New York advertising agency, BBDO. 'The way we would write commercials is the same way we would write songs—we always wanted to write a great song first,' Mary told *Billboard* of the experience in 2012. 'We started writing all these hooks—"next phase, next wave, next craze"—to define what this idea of "Generation Next" meant, and then we kind of went, "Oh, no, the product. We've got to go back and get the product."' The Spice Girls always demanded creative input and equal writing credit on their material; a precedent they were adamant about upholding even for a commercial jingle. 'We had quite good input on it and it's just us lot having a laugh really,' Geri said of the experience. 'We feel it coincides beautifully with Spice Girls. We talk about Girl Power, a new generation, this new feeling, and Pepsi projects the same thing. That's why we decided to do it together.' The Spice Girls were thrilled by the opportunity to record the track at a legendary studio. 'When we recorded "Generation Next Pepsi" we were actually in the studio in Abbey Road where The Beatles wrote their album,' Emma said in *Spiceworld: The Official Book of The Movie*. 'There was even the original piano they used as well. I was telling my uncle about it the other day and he was saying that he used to stand outside and look over the wall just to see where the Beatles recorded [and] I said, "Well I go in there!"'

The girls were enthusiastic about their Pepsi partnership and diligently talked about the cultural significance of the soft drink brand in interviews however in typical Spice-fashion they also drifted from the script at times. When a journalist asked the group what they felt Pepsi could offer them, Mel B comedically jumped in with, 'a lot of money!' She erupted into raucous laughter and the other four girls were unable to keep the smiles from their faces. 'Joke,' Mel B clarified dryly, rearranging her face to appear serious. The Spice Girls Pepsi partnership wasn't novel for a pop act—before their 1997 campaign Pepsi had already run campaigns featuring Michael Jackson, David Bowie, and Madonna and in the years that followed pop behemoths like Beyoncé, Britney Spears, and One Direction got the same treatment. If anything, the campaign solidified the girl group's status as the defining pop act of the moment. There were, however, a few noteworthy aspects to the Spice Girls' Pepsi deal.

Manager Simon Fuller pursued product affiliations that not only benefited the group financially but also boosted the profile of the act at the same time. 'The sponsorship deals were far more about exposure than the money,' he later said of his rationale in David Sinclair's *Wannabe: How The Spice Girls Reinvented Pop*. 'A lot of money was made, but my thinking was if we can get Pepsi to spend $40 million, basically running what was a commercial for my group, then Hallelujah!' As Pepsi used the pop act de-jour to revamp their brand image, the Spice Girls' profile was likewise boosted. 'Everything we do, it's always a two-way thing,' Geri divulged during a day of press in support of their Pepsi campaign. While increased exposure was a driving factor the Spice Girls certainly didn't miss the opportunity for a hefty payday. Simon structured their brand endorsements cleverly so the girls benefitted in the long-term. While a typical licensing deal would have resulted in the band being paid an advance that they would then earn via royalties, typically around 7 per cent of the distributor price, Simon had the act defer advances in favour of a joint partnership. In some cases, the group even contributed to promotional expenses in exchange for a larger share of royalties thereafter. This clever manoeuvre meant their share of profits sometimes climbed as high as 50 per cent. In a November 1997 piece in the business and marketing magazine *Campaign*, writer Ali Qassim credits Pepsi's 'effective use of the all-girl band in a massive promotional campaign' with the record 5 per cent gain in market share the soda producer saw in the summer of 1997 when it clawed sales from competitor Coca-Cola. In exchange, the Spice Girls were paid handsomely and had increased exposure with TV ads airing in 90 countries, Spice Girls-branded Pepsi products on store shelves, a giveaway for an exclusive new song, and a two-night live spectacle is Istanbul sponsored by the soda giant. The mutually beneficial setup was not lost on music critics at the time. 'The Spice Girls wrote a commercial jingle for Pepsi's "Generation Next" ad campaign,' wrote David Plotz in a review of *Spiceworld* for *Slate*. 'Then they included the jingle on *Spiceworld*. You hear the jingle, you buy the album. You buy the album, you hear the jingle. Pepsi sells more Pepsi. The Spice Girls sell more *Spiceworld*. This is what businesspeople call synergy and musicians call prostitution. Whatever it is, it pays.'

The Spice Girls' partnership with Pepsi was also notable because it was occurring simultaneously with a flurry of other product partnerships. In 1997, the band also developed a signature perfumed body spray with Impulse, combined forces with Cadbury for a line of chocolate bars, helped launch a new crisp flavour for Walkers, released a lollipop range with Chupa Chups, unveiled a Spice Cam with Polaroid, and previewed an upcoming *Spice World* game with PlayStation. Their Asda line alone, which launched in time for the 1997 holiday season, included an extensive array of Spice-branded goods for shoppers. You could buy Spice Girls paper plates, birthday cakes, neckties, playing cards, greeting cards, gift wrap, gift tags, banners, handkerchiefs, biscuits, frozen pizzas, Christmas crackers, greeting cards, water bottles, bean bag chairs, puzzles, beach towels, cushions, buttons, T-shirts, sweaters, trackpants, shoes, and balloons, in both rubber and foil varieties. They also had a PMS Stationery line with pens, pencils, pencil cases, sharpeners, erasers, lunch boxes, thermoses, binders, rulers, address books, diaries, keychains, mugs, backpacks, and umbrellas. If your thirst for spicy merchandise still wasn't quenched, you could turn to the Spice Girls-branded bicycles, helmets, in-line skates and bike accessories available through PTI Holdings. The band also published three books in quick succession, had a quarterly magazine, and photo albums and sticker books for the avid collectors. And finally, Galoob's Spice Girls dolls were a must-have item for young fans. This lengthy list is nowhere near comprehensive and doesn't begin to tackle the bootleg products released in tandem, attempting to capitalize on the group's popularity. Young fans ate it all up, eagerly collecting whatever merchandise they could get their hands on. 'I remember feeling an extreme pressure to try and consume everything I could with their picture, the sheer anxiety of seeing magazines and newspapers daily throughout 1997 and trying to decide which was the best to get,' reflected fan Joe Wheeler. 'I certainly wasn't spoilt or a demanding ten-year-old but that burning feeling of missing out on a picture or an article was intense!' At first, Geri's mom tried to collect all the Spice Girls branded products as a hobby but when she realised that it would be impossible to keep up, she threw in the towel.

The band acknowledged that Simon was treading new ground with his Spice Girls merchandising approach. 'He was the first person to really do that, so on one hand, we changed the face of pop music, in terms of marketing and branding,' Mel C noted in her memoir. 'We showed artists that there were other avenues to make money outside of the music itself and traditional merch like t-shirts and badges. And it made us more famous.' But with the unprecedented level of merchandising came repercussions for the band's reputation. 'We were starting to feel like cash machines,' Mel C. 'Sure, we were making money, although not as much as Virgin and 19 were making. But it was our faces over all this stuff, not theirs.' The girls didn't want to be spokeswomen; they wanted to be singers. A ferocious backlash was triggered and Virgin executives admitted internally that perhaps they had been overzealous in their marketing efforts—this would be a contributing factor in the group's decision to part ways with Simon Fuller. Ironically, the Spice Girls agreed with critics who complained that the girl group was inescapable during this period of overexposure. 'We could tell that we were reaching the point of over-saturation. We were everywhere, on everything,' Mel C reflected in *The Sporty One*. 'If I was fed up with seeing us, surely everyone else was too.' It is estimated that the group earned over £300 million in 1997 alone, much of which came from brand deals.

In his review of the *Spiceworld* album, David Browne for *Entertainment Weekly* found the commercial aspect of 'Move Over' off-putting but ultimately succumbed to its poptastic sound. After criticizing the vagueness of the song's lyrics, he paused. 'But then the song's burbling beat kicks in, the Girls' combined voices dig into the "move *over*, yeah/ don't do it *over*, yeah" refrain with the help of a metallic power chord, and suddenly the heart takes over, and you find yourself lying in front of the stereo speakers bowing before the great goddesses of Spice.'

## 'Do It'
Duration: 4:03
Written by Spice Girls, Andy Watkins & Paul Wilson
Produced by Absolute
Engineered by Jeremy Wheatley
Assisted by Jan Kybert
Mixed by Mark 'Spike' Stent
Assisted by Paul 'P.Dub' Walton
Additional programming by Mike Higham
Additional keyboards and programming by Magnus Fiennes
Additional guitar by Milton McDonald
All other instruments by Absolute

'Do It' is a full-throated self-empowerment singalong that imparts listeners with a catchy new mantra while keeping the music as upbeat as the lyrics from the opening notes of piano to the song's fadeout. The Spice Girls deliver a pep talk, the pep talk that they themselves needed in that moment following a year of misogynistic debate about how they should be dressing and acting. The feel-good song provides instructions on how to live life free of the ideological shackles imposed by others.

When the Spice Girls burst onto the scene in the summer of 1996, many were excited by the prospect of a fun new pop act. But others saw them as agents of evil. 'Satan has used the Spice Girls to promote sexual sin, rebellion, witchcraft, pride, immodesty and a host of other destructive practices,' wrote Pastor Joe Schimmel with *Good Fight Ministries*. 'The lyrical content of their songs, as well as their examples as role models, is enough to turn your daughters into tramps just as quickly as the Spice Girls became a sensation.' The band became a 1990s version of the boogeyman, the human embodiment of indecency. With some minidresses, some cleavage, and some curse words, the Spice Girls kickstarted a moral apocalypse and parents fretted about their kids being corrupted by the example set by the Spice Girls. Their clothing was a major point of concern but parents also disapproved of their thrusting dance moves, revisiting the same alarmist sentiments that Elvis generated four decades earlier—in an 1956 review of his appearance on *The Milton Berle Show* his hip-swivelling dance moves were described as 'suggestive and vulgar, tinged with the kind of animalism that should be confined to dives and bordellos'.

In 1997, music producer Phil Spector used his acceptance speech for a *Q* magazine award to tear into the girl group with a degrading rant. 'I was just thinking, are the Spice Girls the Antichrist?' he pondered aloud. 'That's the way it feels to me, there's a big controversy in America right now about them being tantamount to a porno act... Well I disagree with that because there's a big difference between a Spice Girls video and a porno film. Some porno films have pretty good music.' What the Spice Girls did to warrant this comparison is unclear and Phil's stint as an arbiter of decency wouldn't last too long (he died in a prison hospital in 2021 after being convicted of murdering actress Lana Clarkson, his habit of pulling guns on women who rebuffed his advances finally ending in tragedy) but he wasn't alone in feeling that their very existence was obscene. 'I agree with whoever said the Spice Girls are soft porn,' said Radiohead lead singer Thom Yorke in a 1997 interview. 'I don't want any part of it, and if I had kids, I wouldn't want them to have any part of it either.' While men made up the vast majority of those criticising the group, prominent women were also scandalised by the Spice Girls. In January 1997, noted fashion designer Vivienne Westwood appeared on the BBC's *Smillie's People* to share her thoughts. Despite her history of boundary pushing in the fashion industry, including the short-lived operation of a London boutique called SEX that peddled fetish and bondage wear, when it came to the Spice Girls her views were rather conservative. 'What they are marketing is disgusting behaviour as a lifestyle,' she railed, particularly upset that the group was being marketed to young girls. 'People should be outraged by it. I'm morally outraged by it. I call it child molestation. It's corruption.' With some distance from the late 1990s, the outrage seems wildly disproportionate to the way the Spice Girls were actually behaving. Their July 1997 interview with *Rolling Stone* is an apt summation of their antics—they talk about how everyone picks their nose (even President Bill Clinton), they get reprimanded for swearing in an AOL chatroom during a press conference for the brand, they mention that their periods have synchronised, and, yes, they talk a bit about sex but only after the interviewer asked them about it. Chris Heath kickstarted the Q&A asking, 'have you yet been in the position where you're with someone and you wonder if they're thinking, "Wow! I'm having sex with a Spice Girl!?"'

The Spice Girls felt as though they were being set up for failure. In one swift motion, they would be oversexualised and reduced to caricatures of empty-headed sex kittens and then this oversexualisation would be hurled back at them immediately to discredit their music and their message. Emma countered these criticisms saying, 'Just because you've got a short skirt on and a pair of tits, you can still say what you want to say. We're still very strong.' Accusations that they exhibited laddish behaviour shone a light on the real issue—the problem wasn't the behaviour, it was that it was being perpetrated by women.

'Do It' tackles slut-shaming before the term itself even existed— lexicographer Ben Zimmer traces the word's first use back to 2006, however the practice of shaming and shunning someone, typically a woman, for exercising sexual agency was certainly not a new concept. 'Keep your mouth shut, keep your legs shut, get back in your place,' Mel B sings in the song's first verse, parroting the moralistic demands often levied at women. Fifteen years after the Spice Girls wrote these lyrics, a prominent Republican donor in the United States appeared on MSNBC and recommended that women hold an aspirin between their knees as an alternative to contraception, proving that outdated and ignorant ideas have staying power. These vestiges of purity culture maintain that a women's value is tied exclusively to her chastity and feelings of shame can accompany any behaviour that fall outside of a small sliver of acceptability. The Spice Girls always tried to dismantle the notion that there existed only one valid version of womanhood— there are as many possibilities as there are people, and within the band they proudly showcased only five. 'Make your own rules to live by,' the girls harmonise in the pre-chorus of 'Do It'.

If the Spice Girls had let criticism determine how they expressed themselves, their group identity would have felt wooden and inauthentic. But they chose instead to say what they wanted, wear what they wanted, be who they wanted. 'Girl Power is about accepting the way that you are and having fun most importantly,' Victoria said. 'And if you want to wear a short skirt and a Wonderbra wear it but be sure about yourself and basically have a good time.' This approach is what made their legacy one of self-acceptance and embracing individuality. 'Come on and do it / Don't care how you look, it's just how you feel', is advice that prioritises experience over aesthetics.

## 'DENYING'
Duration: 3:46
Written by Spice Girls, Andy Watkins & Paul Wilson
Produced by Absolute
Engineered by Jeremy Wheatley

Assisted by Jan Kybert
Mixed by Mark 'Spike' Stent
Assisted by Paul 'P.Dub' Walton
Additional programming by Mike Higham
Bass by Paul 'Tubbs' Williams
Guitar by Milton McDonald
All other instruments by Absolute

In 'Denying' (the working title of which was 'Ain't Fooling Nobody'), the Spice Girls return to tried-and-tested territory, both musically and conceptually. They deliver a reality check to an out-of-touch lover, informing him that no matter how quick, slick, cool, and smart he considers himself to be, the Spice Girls can effortlessly see through his facade. The persistent synth infuses the track with a distinctly '90s sound while bearing a striking resemblance to another of the band's hits. When *Billboard* revisited *Spiceworld* to mark the album's 20th anniversary, writer Ilana Kaplan highlighted this parallel. '"Denying" always seemed to be the companion piece to *Spice*'s "Say You'll Be There" (not just because of the funk-synth opening),' she wrote. 'And it probably wasn't a coincidence. By this point, it was clear the Spice Girls were saying "ciao" to their denying, lying lover.'

'Denying' was performed consistently during the band's 1998 Spiceworld Tour and the live routine shone a light on the growing chasm between Geri and the rest of the group. The number was staged in a restaurant with Emma seated at a small bistro table serenading a male dancer. Mel C, Mel B, and Victoria performed while exploring the stage. Geri, however, was playing the role of a waitress. With a white apron tied around her waist, she balanced a serving tray of glasses in her right hand while gripping her microphone with her left. To make the balancing act even trickier she'd decided to do the performance in roller-skates. 'She did this whole acting thing as though she was in a major Broadway show and her name was Dizzy Dora The Roller Skater With Her Very Own Spotlight,' Mel B quipped in her memoir *Catch A Fire*. 'You've got to hand it to her, she had big balls, because she couldn't really skate and was uncoordinated.' This lack of coordination proved to be a distraction for the other girls who struggled to focus while Geri wobbled around all over the stage. The illusion of an experienced server was promptly shattered as Geri jolted and tilted her tray at gravity defying angles while attempting to stay upright, revealing that the cups had been glued to the tray's surface. 'I'd be singing away, and suddenly

Geri would be in front of me, gliding precariously back and forth and blocking the audience's view,' Mel B reflected. '"What the fuck is she doing?" I'd think. In the end she was told by the group that she could only skate in one particular area.' Geri herself recalled that during one performance she crashed into the camera operator who was filming footage for the jumbotron.

This conflict was indicative of Geri's greater struggle as a performer—while she was instrumental to the songwriting process and contributed many of the winning ideas that shaped the band's identity, she struggled with the live performance aspects of being a popstar. Choreography was not her strength and she spent much more time rehearsing to attain a level of comfort that seemed natural to the other girls. 'She sometimes felt vulnerable onstage, even though she always pulled it off because she worked so hard to get it right,' Mel C later wrote about her struggling friend. This extra work and a feeling of inadequacy left Geri exhausted and depressed. The four other Spice Girls took notice of Geri's withdrawn behaviour as well as some drastic fluctuations in weight but chalked it up to her demanding schedule. But internally, Geri was crumbling under the pressure. The tour consisted of 97 shows across Europe and North America, a daunting concept when she already felt strained after the first dozen. 'In retrospect, it was clear Geri was unhappy and that something was amiss,' Mel C reflected. 'She became very quiet and withdrawn, no longer that energetic young woman with loads of mad ideas and an insatiable drive to push the band to greater and greater heights. She withdrew.' Following Geri's departure from the Spice Girls in May 1998, 'Denying' remained part of the core setlist but no longer featured a waitress, roller-skating or otherwise. It has not been performed live by the group since the conclusion of the 1998 tour.

## 'Viva Forever'
Duration: 5:10
Written by Spice Girls, Matt Rowe & Richard Stannard
Produced by Richard Stannard & Matt Rowe
Recorded and engineered by Adrian Bushby
Mixed by Mark 'Spike' Stent
Assisted by Paul 'P.Dub' Walton
Keyboards and programming by Matt Rowe
Additional programming by Pete Davis

Additional engineering by Jake Davies
Acoustic guitar by John Themis
Strings arranged by Anne Dudley
Released as a single 20 July 1998

Due to the monumental changes that the band endured at the time of its release, 'Viva Forever' is an emotionally loaded Spice Girls track. When they began promoting it, they were whole and, from the outside perspective of fans, all was right in Spiceworld. But by the time the single was formally released, the band had lost one of their own and the girl group was forever changed. Originally written as a bittersweet reflection on a waning summer romance, the song now served as a eulogy for the end of a creative partnership and, more importantly, a friendship. Geri's shocking departure from the Spice Girls generated waves of devastation for young fans around the world and 'Viva Forever' served as the poignant soundtrack to their heartache. The song's melancholic tone, complete with fluttering flamenco guitars and aching lyrics, fit the turmoil of the moment so impeccably that the drama inadvertently doubled as promotion for the single, propelling it to the top of the charts. 'Viva Forever' serves as a demarcation point for the Spice Girls, the dividing line of before and after—it was the last song Geri performed with the Spice Girls on television before she quit and, likewise, it was the first song the group performed without her as a newly established foursome.

Geri pinpoints one final incident as her impetus to leave. On 26 May 1998, the *Sun* ran a story with the headline 'Ginger Spice Secret Breast Cancer Op'. When Geri was 17 years old, she underwent emergency surgery to remove a lump from her breast and then anxiously waited for results to determine next steps—if the cells were cancerous a mastectomy may have been needed. Fortunately, the growth was benign and Geri was able to begin young adulthood in good health. While the media ran this story without her consent, she felt that she should take advantage of the opportunity to educate young women about breast health. She secured an interview with *ITN*'s *News at Ten* who were willing to fly a crew out to Helsinki, Finland where the Spice Girls were performing on tour. 'I felt especially enthusiastic. The *ITN* late evening news reached a large audience and only did serious pieces. I could make an important point about breast cancer and warn young women of the need to be vigilant,' Geri recalled in her memoir.

But the interview didn't happen. According to Geri, it was stopped dead when the band decided that she shouldn't make a solo appearance—the

Spice Girls came as a packaged deal. Geri was deflated. 'That kind of did it for me,' she said. 'I thought, I can't even do that by myself.' While the breast cancer campaign may have been the tipping point it was far from the only thing weighing on Geri at the time. Her other grievances, barely held in check at this point, bubbled to the surface—an overpacked work schedule, a physically demanding tour, a snowballing eating disorder, and complicated interpersonal band dynamics all contributed to Geri's emotional state. 'I say it was because they didn't want me to do this breast cancer interview alone [...] but you know that was kind of the final straw,' she reflected with some distance from the situation in the 2007 BBC documentary *Spice Girls: Giving You Everything*. 'I just felt like I didn't belong anymore. They didn't need me anymore really and I definitely felt very redundant. The wheels were turning whether I was there or not.'

In her final television appearance with the Spice Girls on *Top of the Pops*, Geri appears withdrawn and is a ghost of the Ginger Spice who once dominated appearances with loud interjections, witty comments, and a beaming smile. Her fiery red hair had faded into a more subdued shade of strawberry blonde and her fabulous stage costuming was nowhere to be found. Instead, she wore a buttoned-up cardigan and a long skirt that swallowed her tiny frame. Dressed in head to toe black as though headed to a funeral, she seemed to be willing herself to fade into the background, the light behind her eyes gone. Her performance is sullen and lifeless and the camera skims over her quickly, focusing on the other girls who are engaged in the song. '"Viva Forever" is probably one of the saddest songs for me because I remember when I was on stage with [the other girls] and I kind of knew I'd had enough,' Geri lamented. 'I was standing there thinking, oh my god, this is the last time I'm going to sing this with these girls. I can't do it anymore. I just felt empty and like I'd given them everything I could.' As the five girls swayed in unison for the final time the lyrics to Geri's swan song were befitting. 'Slippin' through our fingers, like the sands of time / Promises made, every memory saved / As reflections in my mind', Mel C sings in the second verse.

On the morning of 27 May, the Spice Girls assembled to begin another busy day but Geri didn't turn up. As the other four girls waited in confusion, they received a phone call from their lawyer: Geri was done. They were stunned. 'The last time I saw Geri was on the flight from Helsinki,' Victoria reflected in *Learning To Fly*. 'I remember that flight because we were all in such good spirits [and] I remember laughing so much it hurt. Then we hugged and said see you tomorrow and that was it. I had no idea. Literally no idea.' Emma recalls their final flight together as well but in hindsight noticed signs that something was amiss. 'Me and Geri were actually sitting opposite each other,' Emma shared. 'We'd landed and Geri got up and went "I'm going to say goodbye girls" and I thought well that's really weird. We never say goodbye to each other because we'd go home for a couple hours and then be back together.' Mel C offhandedly noted that Geri's formal farewells were strange but just shrugged it off. Now, just a few hours later, their world had been turned upside down and they were reanalysing every minor detail about the night prior.

The Spice Girls forged ahead with the day's scheduled events and made an appearance on *The National Lottery*. They sang 'Viva Forever' which conveniently had no solo lines by Geri so it was a relatively smooth transition. 'Let's just say she's ill and just feel it out for a minute to see if she's going to come back at all,' Mel B explained of the band's mindset at the time in *Giving You Everything*. 'That's what I was hoping for anyway.' Although panicked internally, Mel C put on a brave face and fibbed to host Carol Smilie on live TV saying that Geri was unwell. She turned directly to the camera and sent a message to Geri. 'Get well soon!' But as the hours dragged on, the reality of the situation began to set in. Geri was not returning.

Over the next 48 hours the remaining four Spice Girls repeatedly dialled Geri begging for her to return while also discussing legal recourse with lawyers but after two days of stalling, and two short-staffed gigs in Oslo, Norway, Geri released a statement through her lawyer on 31 May 1998. 'Sadly, I would like to confirm that I have left the Spice Girls. This is because of differences between us. I'm sure the group will continue to be successful and I wish them all the best. I have no immediate plans. I wish to apologise to all the fans and to thank them and everyone who's been there. Lots of love, Geri. P.S. I'll be back.'

The generation of fans who believed the Spice Girls implicitly when they promised that friendship would never end were left crushed by Geri's exit. For many in the young fanbase, it was their first brush with heartbreak and the disappointment stung. Teary-eyed kids clutched their Spice Girls merchandise close and watched the evening news praying that there had been some kind of mistake. The emotions of that day still live just below the surface for many who feel they never recovered from Geri's betrayal. Some refer to it as the worst day of their childhoods without a hint of irony. In discussions of the topic, the word 'traumatising' is thrown about frequently. 'This was the day I experienced my first heartbreak, at 6 years old,' reflected lifelong fan Amanda in 2024. 'I sobbed for days afterward.' Aside from unleashing a torrent of anguish from young millennials, there were also very real business impacts as well. Virgin EMI Records saw their shares decrease by 3.1 per cent on the London Stock Exchange following Geri's departure as investors feared the label's best-selling act was about to crumble.

Meanwhile the tabloids went into overdrive. The press already dissected the band's every move and stirred up drama wherever possible to produce the most salacious headline—now that an actual bombshell had been dropped, they were using the opportunity to speculate wildly on the inner workings of the band. For months they had been suggesting that a band breakup was imminent because of mounting tensions within the girl group, specifically between Mel B and Geri. Now that Geri had walked out rumours were running wild. 'It's no secret that [Geri] and Melanie have had a very fiery relationship in the past,' Mel C later said, confirming that that the gossip was rooted in fact. 'They're the closest of all of the band, they're absolutely in each other's pockets. Or they can fight like cat and dog. They're very much the strongest characters in the band in many ways so that really changed the dynamic on a day-to-day basis sometimes.' During a 2019 appearance *Piers Morgan's Life Stories*, Mel B divulged that she and Geri briefly had a sexual relationship, something that could have further complicated their dynamic. When the pair were in synch, their enthusiasm and decisiveness made the band stronger—they could combine forces to bring ideas to life. This fire made the Spice Girls exceptional. When they were at odds, however, band morale deteriorated. If they disagreed carnage ensued, sometimes literally as Mel C recalled one time when Geri got 'clocked in the face'. Shouting matches were not uncommon. 'There was definitely friction in the relationship between Melanie [Brown] and I,' Geri corroborated. 'She knows that. And I found it increasingly difficult.' But for every kernel of truth that appeared in the papers in 1998, something ludicrous was printed as well—one publication claimed that Geri's interest in the occult drove a wedge between her and her bandmates.

As the world reeled, so did the remaining members of the band. 'We'd made a pact, me and her, that if she wanted to leave, she'd tell me or if I wanted to leave, I'd tell her,' Mel B explained. 'And she just left. All of a sudden, just vanished. It was really, really upsetting for me.' Emma was likewise distressed. 'Personally, I was distraught. I was so upset,' Emma said. 'But professionally we had to make it work, we had to move on, move forward.' The girls were not afforded much time to process the grief of losing a colleague and best friend in one fell swoop—the American leg of their world tour loomed and there was a lot of work to do. 'We have a whole show to do with one person missing,' Mel B stressed. 'We now have to re-choreograph the dance routines and dish out the lyrics and the lines. My brain automatically went to that.'

Months before Geri quit, the busy band had opted to produce a stop-motion animated music video for 'Viva Forever'. It was originally planned for a May 1998 release as a double A-side single with 'Never Give Up on the Good Times' but after several delays the double A-side concept was abandoned. When 'Viva Forever' was finally released on 20 July 1998, it was a little disorienting to see an animated version of Geri still tagging along happily with the other four girls. The band appeared as fairies, personified by 12-inch malleable puppets crafted by animator Steve Box. At the time, he was working for Aardman Animations, later responsible for the critically revered stop-motion *Wallace & Gromit* series. 'I came up with this idea for the girls to be tin toy fairies that were like lost toys,' Steve explained in a 2017 interview with Ruby Lott-Lavigna of *Crack* magazine. He pulled inspiration from the children's books he was reading to his young kids, specifically *Rupert Bear*. 'Often Rupert comes across some weird living toy in the woods or some secret doorway in a tree,' Steve remarked. 'They're quite surreal stories, quite magical.' The Spice Girls puppets achieved the enchanted effect Steve was chasing, although there was also something unsettling about them—their furrowed brows made them look a little cross, their smiles were slightly too wide, and their eyes occasionally flashed with a devious glint. Their uncanny air only accentuated the other mysteries of the video's narrative. Two children walk through an open field and encounter the Spice fairies, then one kid is imprisoned inside a Rubik's Cube that gets swallowed into a gumball machine. The video concludes and the trapped child is never seen again. 'It's like the sadness of the song is leaving your childhood behind,' Steve elaborated. 'Pop music is all about sex and love, so becoming interested in that, you suddenly put the toys away, you start to grow up in a different way.' The video perfectly complements the sadness-tinged track and serves as an otherworldly reflection on love and loss, beginnings and endings.

'Viva Forever' sold 278,000 copies in the first week of release and debuted at No. 1 in the UK where it became the Spice Girls' seventh No. 1 single. Continuing a great tradition, critics were once again split on the track, with some dismissing it as cheesy and others describing it as a haunting summer ballad. Despite the turmoil surrounding its release, it has endured as a fan favourite and was performed live during all four Spice Girls tours. On the 1998 Spiceworld Tour, 'Viva Forever' was preceded by a prescient audio excerpt from Ridley Scott's 1982

The Spice Girls photographed for their debut album in Tokyo, Japan in May 1996. (*Brittany Smith / Alamy Stock Photo*)

The Spice Girls at the Hallam FM Party in the Park in Sheffield in August 1996. (*Brittany Smith / Alamy Stock Photo*)

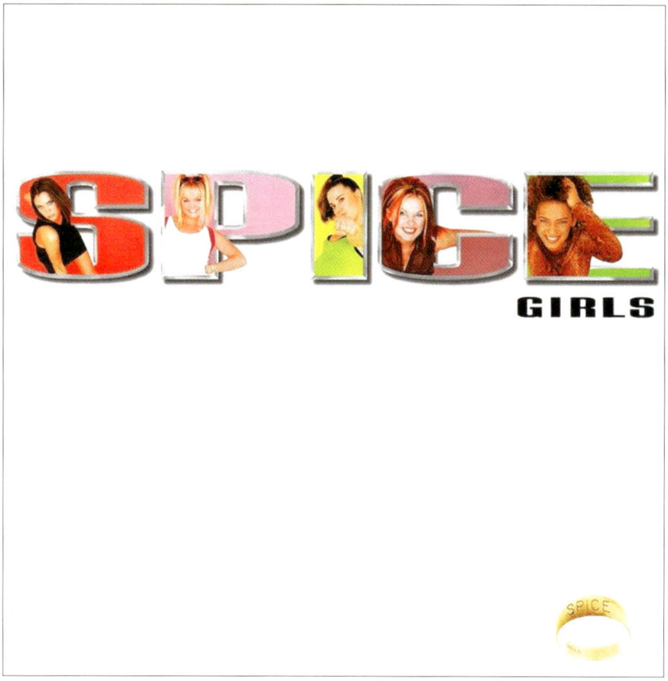

*Left:* The Spice Girls' debut album *Spice* has sold over 23 million copies globally and remains the best-selling album ever released by a girl group. (*Copyright Virgin Records Ltd.*)

*Opposite:* 'Who Do You Think You Are' was the official Comic Relief single of 1997. (*Trinity Mirror / Mirrorpix / Alamy Stock Photo*)

The Spice Girls perform at a Billboard event in Los Angeles, California. (*Pictorial Press / Alamy Stock Photo*)

The Spice Girls gave a decade defining performance at the 1997 BRIT Awards. (*Fiona Hanson / PA Images / Alamy Stock Photo*)

The Spice Girls arrive at the Cannes Film Festival in May 1997 to announce their upcoming feature film. (*John Ferguson / Trinity Mirror / Mirrorpix / Alamy Stock Photo*)

Victoria photographed with new beau, David Beckham, at her parents' home in Hertfordshire after a romantic getaway in Italy. (*Trinity Mirror / Mirrorpix / Alamy Stock Photo*)

The Spice Girls shot *Spice World The Movie* between June and August 1997 while also writing and recording their sophomore album. (*Spice Productions / AJ Pics / Alamy Stock Photo*)

In the summer of 1997, the Spice Girls participated in a Pepsi advertising campaign, one of many brand deals for the girl group. (*Isabel Infantes / Alamy Stock Photo*)

The Spice Girls were everywhere in the summer of 1997, including the July edition of *Rolling Stone*. (*Ralf Liebhold / Dreamstime.com*)

*Above:* The Spice Girls were presented with a plaque commemorating sales of 18 million for *Spice* within a year while visiting Granada, Spain in October 1997. (*PA Images / Alamy Stock Photo*)

*Below:* Galoob's Spice Girls dolls were a must-have item for young fans. (*Ben Curtis / PA Images / Alamy Stock Photo*)

The Spice Girls visited Pretoria, South Africa to meet Nelson Mandela with Prince Charles in November 1997. (*Trinity Mirror / Mirrorpix / Alamy Stock Photo*)

The Spice Girls' second album, *Spiceworld*, was released in the UK on 4 November 1997 and debuted at No. 1. (*Copyright Virgin Records Ltd*)

*Above:* The Spice Girls at the MTV Europe Awards in Holland in November 1997, accepting the award for Best Group. Back in New York manager Simon Fuller was being fired. (Fabio Diena / Dreamstime.com)

*Right:* Spice World The Movie was released in the UK on 26 December 1997. It had a strong box office performance despite poor reviews. (Copyright PolyGram Filmed Entertainment)

The Spice Girls didn't do anything without an obsessed tabloid press following their every move. (*Trinity Mirror / Mirrorpix / Alamy Stock Photo*)

In February 1998, the Spice Girls embarked on a 97-date sold-out world tour. (*Sean Dempsey / PA Images / Alamy Stock Photo*)

*Above:* The Spice Girls performing 'Naked' in Glasgow, Scotland in April 1998. (*Trinity Mirror / Mirrorpix / Alamy Stock Photo*)

*Right:* Melanie Brown with tour dancer Jimmy Gulzar. The pair would soon marry and have a daughter. (*Bill Belknap / Alamy Stock Photo*)

Under mounting pressure and a relentless schedule, Geri began to withdraw. (*David Kendall / PA Images / Alamy Stock Photo*)

Geri's lawyer confirms her departure from the Spice Girls on 31 May 1998, kicking off a media frenzy. (*Trinity Mirror / Mirrorpix / Alamy Stock Photo*)

The Spice Girls carried on as a four-piece for the North American leg of the tour. (*PA / Alamy Stock Photo*)

The Spice Girls photographed with Prince Charles at the 77th Royal Variety Performance. Both Mel B and Victoria were now pregnant. (*John Stillwell / PA Images / Alamy Stock Photo*)

As 1998 wound down, Spice-related work was handled by Emma and Mel C to allow pregnant Mel B and Victoria some time off. (*Hartwig Valdmanis / United Archives GmbH / Alamy Stock Photo*)

Victoria and fiancé David Beckham photographed at an *Aida* launch event with Sir Elton John and Sir Tim Rice. (*Tony Harris / PA Images / Alamy Stock Photo*)

The Spice Girls returned after a two-year absence with their third album, *Forever*, in November 2000. (*Copyright Virgin Records Ltd*)

The Spice Girls performed 'Holler' at the MTV European Music Awards in 2000—this would be their last public appearance as a group until their 2007 reunion. (*Harvey Anthony Harvey / PA Images / Alamy Stock Photo*)

In June 2007, all five Spice Girls gathered at London's O2 Arena to hold a press conference announcing a world tour and *Greatest Hits* album. (*Rune Hellestad / UPI / Alamy Stock Photo*)

All five Spice Girls last performed together at the Closing Ceremony of the 2012 London Olympics. (*Allstar Picture Library Ltd / Alamy Stock Photo*)

science fiction film *Blade Runner*. 'The light that burns twice as bright burns half as long, and you have burned so very very brightly, Roy,' says actor Joe Turkel.

The Spice Girls wrote 'Viva Forever' with Matt and Biff in the summer of 1997. They came straight from the film set and descended on Abbey Road Studios in a whirlwind, scattered and distracted because of another crazy day. Biff finally snapped. 'I remember stopping the session and raising my voice a little bit,' he recalled in a 2020 discussion with Mel C on a YouTube Live Q&A. He and Matt had shown the girl group great patience as they balanced the movie and the album but the atmosphere was too chaotic to get any work done and something needed to change. Biff expressed his frustration. 'The room is too big, it's too flash, it's Abbey Road. We need to go somewhere in a small room and sit on the floor and write a song,' he told the girls. 'And then two or three hours later we'd written 'Viva Forever.' Once separated from distraction the song materialised quickly. The lyrics were written almost entirely by Geri, so the song was a fitting send off as her last single as a Spice Girl. The working title of the song was simply 'Obrigado', Portuguese for 'Thank You'.

## 'THE LADY IS A VAMP'
Duration: 3:10
Written by Spice Girls, Andy Watkins & Paul Wilson
Produced by Absolute
Orchestral arrangement by Steve Sidwell
Engineered by Jeremy Wheatley and Mark Tucker
Assisted by Jan Kybert and Stephen Pelluet
Mixed by Mark 'Spike' Stent
Assisted by Paul 'P.Dub' Walton
Additional programming by Mike Higham

'The Lady is a Vamp' is an audacious 1930s swing pastiche that closes *Spiceworld* with an appropriately theatrical finale. The song's title is a reference to the song 'The Lady is a Tramp' from the 1937 musical *Babes in Arms* which the Spice Girls directly address and correct, asserting that 'the lady is a vamp, she's a vixen not a tramp'. It is a celebration of old Hollywood that namechecks pop culture icons, both real and fictional, who have remained relevant and recognizable long after their heydays: Elvis Presley, Bob Marley, Charlie's Angels, Twiggy, Jackie O, and Marilyn Monroe are just some of the famous faces revered in the number. The Spice

Girls can be seen dressing up as most of the referenced celebrities during a photoshoot montage in *Spice World The Movie*. The song concludes with the Spice Girls' famous nicknames being added to the list of legendary figures: 'Scary, Baby, Ginger, Posh, Sporty, yes, now that's your lot.'

These monikers were culturally ubiquitous just a few months into the Spice Girls' reign as pop darlings however the band had no hand in selecting them. The nicknames developed organically in July 1996 following the release of 'Wannabe' when writer Peter Lorraine featured the group in *Top of the Pops* magazine with a playful graphic captioned 'Spice Rack!' A set of five spice jars were arranged in a row, a photo of a Spice Girl attached to each and labelled with an accompanying nickname. 'I had an editorial meeting back at the office and about four of us started thinking of names,' Peter remembered in a 2015 *Stylist* interview. 'Posh was the first one to be thought up because Victoria looks pretty sophisticated. The rest were pretty easy really because the girls' characters were already really strong.' Jennifer Cawthron, one of the writers helping Peter brainstorm, remembers the process being quick and easy. 'The girls were already like cartoon characters of themselves, so it only took about ten seconds to come up with the nicknames,' she shared. 'Victoria was Posh Spice because she was wearing Gucci and seemed pouty and reserved. Emma wore pigtails and sucked a lollipop, so obviously she was Baby Spice. Mel C spent the whole time leaping around in her tracksuit so we called her Sporty Spice. I named Mel B Scary Spice because she was so shouty. And Geri was Ginger Spice simply because of her hair. Not much thought went into that one.' A couple of alternate pitches, such as Scouse Spice for Mel C and Saucy Spice for Geri, quickly fell by the wayside.

The Spice Girls weren't just content with the nicknames, they were thrilled. 'The tags were a marketing man's dream,' Geri exclaimed in *If Only*. 'From that moment on, we began using them as alternative names.' The labels felt comfortable for the girls immediately because they aligned with their pre-existing styles and personalities. They leaned into them even harder. 'Our characters became more and more cartoon-like. My hair became redder, my lipstick brighter and my outfits more outlandish,' Geri continued. It's hard to imagine the band without the nicknames, a testament to their lasting power. 'Although it might seem obvious now, it wasn't then,' Victoria remarked in her memoir. 'We were just Geri, Melanie, Melanie, Emma and Victoria.'

The nicknames helped endear the band to fans who felt represented within the line-up. It became common to identify as one of the Spice Girls, with fans enthusiastically stating, 'I'm such a Sporty Spice!' or 'I'm more of a Baby than a Ginger'. The catchy names stuck in the public's consciousness. 'Everyone loves nicknames—nicknames make you feel closer to someone and it was really something that the kids could identify with—from the start they would pick one of us and dress like us,' Victoria reasoned. It also helped launch the girls into the tabloids as fully formed characters, and while the resulting media harassment wasn't a welcome by-product the press attention certainly helped boost the band's profile. 'In the same way that we decided to embrace our individual style, the names also just happened to become a big part of our success,' Mel C shared in her autobiography. 'There wasn't anything cynical in it. There were no chats with a marketing team, no one held a focus group. It was just a joke for a magazine that ended up brilliantly defining us to each other and our fans.' While detractors at the time felt it was deluded and narcissistic for the Spice Girls to list themselves as counterparts of Elvis Presley and Marilyn Monroe, in the decades since 'The Lady is a Vamp' was written the band's standing as 'legends built to last' has only been reinforced by their continued significance.

The song was written with Absolute on the set of *Spice World The Movie* and while the filming schedule was hectic for the girl group there was one member in particular who was always dedicated to developing new material with a signature Spice flair. '"The Lady is a Vamp" was totally with Geri,' Andy revealed.

4

# Non-Album Tracks
# 1997–1998

'SPICE INVADERS'
Duration: 3:38
Written by Spice Girls, Andy Watkins & Paul Wilson
Produced by Absolute
Mixed by Jeremy Wheatley
Released as a B-side with 'Spice Up Your Life' on 13 October 1997

No song in the Spice Girls catalogue better captures the essence of a depleted band than 'Spice Invaders'. As Virgin Records geared up for the release of *Spiceworld*'s lead single, 'Spice Up Your Life', there was still no accompanying B-side. With the Spice Girls running low on time, material, and energy after an overscheduled summer Andy Watkins helped them cobble together a slapdash number. 'We set up four microphones and recorded them all talking to each other and then we put some hideous bubblegum backing track down behind their voices and just somehow pieced it all together,' he said. The results are some stream-of-consciousness musings from five exhausted women over sporadic strums of a sitar, a punchy beat, and aimless whistling. 'This song is full of valid information, information like never wee with your knickers on,' Mel B says. 'I should be over there eating my sweets, I think,' Emma interjects offhandedly, making no attempt to disguise her disinterest in the track. When she later wonders aloud where Geri and Mel are, Victoria provides a depressing but likely truthful answer: 'I think they're asleep.' The production team tried desperately to massage the vocal recordings into a track with some substance which proved to be a time-consuming endeavour. Andy had to leave in the middle of mixing when his wife went into labour—after his baby boy arrived safely, he returned to the studio to find engineer Jeremy Wheatley understandably stumped by the track.

On 8 November 2018, music critic Alexis Petridis wrote a piece for *The Guardian* ranking all of the Spice Girls songs and, uncontroversially, 'Spice Invaders' came dead last. 'This B-side consists of the band members talking, albeit quite wittily over a very 1998 spoof spy-film soundtrack backdrop,' he wrote. 'It is the sound of a group who could, by this point, get away with anything.'

## 'WALK OF LIFE'
Duration: 4:16
Written by Spice Girls, Andy Watkins & Paul Wilson
Produced by Absolute
Mixed by Tom Elmhurst
Released as a B-side with 'Too Much' on 15 December 1997

'Walk of Life' is reggae love letter to the ever-bustling City of London in which the Spice Girls memorialize the unfaltering energy of the city's parks, pubs, clubs, and landmarks. The track is a fittingly breezy tribute to a town where, consistently, the 'vibe is right'. It was released as a B-side to 'Too Much' in December 1997 in most markets however its NortWh American release was delayed until 27 October 1998, when it was included on the TV soundtrack *Sabrina the Teenage Witch: The Album*. In 2013, the song's co-writer, Andy Watkins, confirmed that even just a few weeks prior to release 'Walk of Life' was set to be included as an eleventh track on *Spiceworld* but it was removed with no replacement for unknown reasons.

A shortened version of the song was incorporated into early stops on the 1998 Spiceworld Tour, giving the Spice Girls the opportunity to salute the local crowd by swapping out references to London for the city they were visiting. Clad in crushed velvet jumpsuits, the girls were scooped up by musclebound Spice Boys for some dramatic choreography—they were tossed about and hoisted up on the male dancers' shoulders to strike poses before being carried off stage as the relaxed beat persisted. Due to the physical nature of the dance routine, it was shelved for the final two months of shows after both Mel B and Victoria became pregnant.

## 'OUTER SPACE GIRLS'
Duration: 3:58
Written by Spice Girls, Matt Rowe & Richard Stannard
Produced by Matt Rowe & Richard Stannard
Mixed by Mark 'Spike' Stent
Released as a B-side with 'Too Much' on 15 December 1997

With 'Outer Space Girls' the Spice Girls broaden their original goal of world domination to focus instead on conquering the totality of the universe. Written in the summer of 1997, the song's subject matter echoes multiple plot points in *Spice World The Movie*, demonstrating that the band was drawing from the same wells of inspiration on set and in the studio. Mel C sings about the 'Spice Force 5 singing 'Wannabe', a nod to both the band's debut hit and a sequence from the movie—Spice Force 5 is an idea pitched by Hollywood film producers who want the Spice Girls to star in a feature film as a team of expert operatives who excel in martial arts, espionage, explosives, disguise, and being generally fabulous. Geri later delivers lyrics about, 'Close encounters of the female kind', a Girl Power-infused reference to the 1977 Steven Spielberg sci-fi blockbuster *Close Encounters of the Third Kind* which tells the story of a typical middle-American man whose life is turned upside down after a UFO encounter. The Spice Girls have their own UFO encounter in the film when they meet some handsy aliens who are desperate for autographs, concert tickets, and selfies.

'Outer Space Girls' is a distillation of '90s production trends held together by a zappy electronic beat and funky rocketing baseline. Record scratches, robotic voice modulation, and twinkling galactic sound effects are thrown in for good measure to deliver a kitschy and fun dance track about whizzing through space.

## 'AIN'T NO STOPPING US NOW'
Duration: 4:55
Featuring Luther Vandross
Written by Gene McFadden, John Whitehead, and Jerry Cohen
Produced by Mike Higham
Engineered by Andy Gallimore
Released as a B-side with 'Stop' on 9 March 1998

'Ain't No Stopping Us Now' is a disco track originally recorded in 1979 by Gene McFadden, John Whitehead, and keyboardist Jerry Cohen.

Hailing from Philadelphia, Pennsylvania, McFadden & Whitehead were inspired to write the song after emerging victorious from a power struggle with their record label, but its message of jubilant resilience saw it embraced as an anthem in the fight against the racial discrimination that tyrannised the African American community.

On 9 November 1997, the Spice Girls recorded *An Audience with the Spice Girls*, an hour-long TV special filmed in front of a star-studded and all-female studio audience. The band fielded questions from the audience of young fans (and the likes of Jennifer Saunders, Twiggy, and Lorraine Kelly) and performed seven of their hit songs. Midway through the show, they announced a special guest. 'There's one person we've always wanted to sing with,' Emma told the buzzing crowd. 'Janet Jackson got to sing with him, Mariah Carey got to sing with him, and now it's our chance. We are honoured and thrilled to welcome Mr. Luther Vandross!' Nicknamed "The Velvet Voice", renowned soul artist Luther Vandross released *Songs* in 1994, an album featuring covers of 13 timeless classic, one of which was 'Ain't No Stopping Us Now'. 'We're going to sing a song and we're going to really spice it up!' he exclaimed before launching into the number with the Spice Girls. The program aired on 29 November 1997 and over 12 million people across the UK tuned in to watch. A recording of the performance was included as a B-side to 'Stop' four months later.

## '(How Does It Feel to Be) On Top of the World'
Duration: 4:50
Written by Ian McCulloch and Johnny Marr
Produced by Ian McCulloch
Engineered and mixed by Alan Douglas
Executive produced by Paul Toogood
Released as a single by England United on 1 June 1998

In July 1965, the official mascot of the 1966 FIFA World Cup was unveiled to be World Cup Willie, a lion with a union jack emblazoned on his jersey to commemorate England's hosting role. Leading up to the tournament, this character appeared in comic strips, made live television appearances, was featured on an expansive line of merchandise, and was even the subject of the tournament's official anthem written by Scottish folk singer-songwriter Lonnie Donegan. The song, aptly titled 'World Cup Willie', became an endearing part of England's matches and when the team defeated West Germany in the final their triumph was attributed, in part, to the passionate support of their fanbase, something World Cup Willie was credited with bolstering. When the 1970 World Cup was held in Mexico four years later, an official England national football team song was developed to try and recapture that same winning magic. The tradition of a team song has been upheld ever since.

'(How Does It Feel to Be) On Top of the World' was written by Echo and the Bunnymen frontman Ian McCulloch and The Smiths' founding member and guitarist, Johnny Marr. The first iteration of the song was written in 1993 for a BBC football documentary series but it was resurrected, submitted, and selected as the England team's official song for the 1998 World Cup, allegedly beating submissions from Blur, Pulp, and The Lightning Seeds in the process. In February 1998, the sample song was re-recorded by a supergroup called England United comprised of four British bands: Echo and the Bunnymen, Ocean Colour Scene, Space, and the Spice Girls. The four acts came together in a London studio space on 18 April 1998 to star in a music video that highlighted the sport's intergenerational appeal by having young, football-playing children morph into the adult musicians featured on the track. The video also features cameos from National Team players Ian Wright, Rio Ferdinand and David Beckham. The single, particularly the video, features Geri Halliwell prominently but was released just a day after her departure from the Spice Girls was confirmed.

'(How Does It Feel to Be) On Top of the World' is not a particularly beloved team song and was largely overshadowed during the tournament by some unofficial releases. 'Vindaloo' by Fat Les was an infectious parody of football anthems featuring lyrics by comedian Keith Allen and music by bassist Guy Pratt and Alex James from Blur. The exceptionally singable track eclipsed England United's more earnest Brit pop offering that wasn't conducive to crowd singalongs. Likewise, 'Three Lions' by The Lightning Seeds with lyrics by comedians David Baddiel and Frank Skinner was originally written for the 1996 UEFA European Championship and was revamped for the 1998 World Cup. With the refrain 'Football's coming home' acting as the song's anchor, the tune was a wistful yet optimistic soundtrack to the tournament. 'Vindaloo' peaked at No. 2 on the charts while 'Three Lions '98' clung to the top spot for three full weeks. Meanwhile '(How Does It Feel to Be) On Top of the World' debuted at No. 9 before promptly tumbling.

# 5

# *Goodbye*

The Spice Girls released *Goodbye* on 14 December 1998 and it became the fastest-selling single of 1998 and the best-selling British single of 1998. The song 'Goodbye' became the band's eighth No. 1 single and their third consecutive Christmas No. 1, matching the record previously set by The Beatles. In addition to 'Goodbye', the band's EP included three covers, one recorded in studio and two recorded live at London's Wembley Stadium in September 1998.

'Goodbye'
Duration: 4:44
Written by Spice Girls, Matt Rowe & Richard Stannard
Produced by Matt Rowe & Richard Stannard
Mixed by Mark 'Spike' Stent
Assisted by Jan Kybert and Paul 'P.Dub' Walton
Engineered by Adrian Bushby
Additional engineering by Jake Davies
Drum programming by Paul Waller
Strings arranged by Will Malone
Released as a single on 14 December 1998

In July 1998, Biff Stannard and Matt Rowe exchanged England's rainy weather for the thick summer heat and humidity of Nashville, Tennessee. As the Spice Girls approached the halfway mark of their North American tour, they were making a transitory stop in Nashville for a sold-out show at the Starwood Amphitheater but had carved out some time with their steadfast co-writers to work on a new song. The group gathered in Nashville's Music Row district at Ocean Way, a recording studio housed in a century-old gothic church where the high ceilings and stone walls created exemplary acoustics and the space's peaceful ambiance stoked inspiration. For a song largely about change, the lofty workspace underlined just how much their lives had been transformed over the course of three years. '[It] was a proper "God, can you believe we're here?" moment,' Biff marvelled in David Sinclair's *Wannabe: How The Spice Girls Reinvented Pop*. 'It was an amazing, super-posh studio. We finished writing the song and they sang it.'

The song's development had begun thousands of miles away in a different country, in a different year, when the Spice Girls themselves were a different band. 'I was there when they wrote it,' Geri revealed in a 1999 interview with *Much Music*. The song was first conceived at a session at London's Abbey Road Studios during the development of *Spiceworld* and featured lyrics written primarily by Geri and Emma over a simple piano backing. It is rumoured that it began as a tribute to the victims of the 1996 Dunblane massacre but when the remaining four Spice Girls revisited the track the next summer, it underwent a significant rewrite and all lyrical contributions from Geri were discarded along with the original subject matter. The Spice Girls were in a period of flux and the track became a bittersweet send-off to a bygone era. 'It's goodbye to the past and hello to the future,' the Spice Girls said frequently of the song's theme while promoting it. But many fans could only interpret the track as a goodbye to one person: Geri.

'We write [about] what we've been through and obviously when we wrote the song, we did have Geri in mind,' Emma said in a December 1998 appearance on *Skattefri Lørdag*. 'It's something we wanted to do. The lyrics are beautiful and we're really proud of it.' Emma was devastated by Geri's abrupt departure and struggled to mentally separate the severing of a business relationship from the dissolution of their personal bond. 'I found that whole process very difficult because it was more like oh my god, she's walked out on a friendship,' Emma later reflected in 2012's *The Spice Girls Story: Viva Forever!* documentary. 'That's the only way I saw it. I didn't see it as walking out on a career. I just saw it as my friend has gone.' With 'Goodbye' the Spice Girls were able to mourn Geri's departure beside the fans who shared their heartbreak. 'Just a little girl, big imagination / Never letting no one take it away / Went into the world, what a revelation / She found there's a better way for you and me to be', Emma sings in the song's second verse, honouring Geri's creativity and drive.

While Geri's absence undeniably weighed heavily on the band at the time, not everyone saw the track as being about her and her alone. 'If you look at it now, you could say ["Goodbye"] was about Geri,' Biff told Christopher Barrett of *Music Week* in November 2007. 'But I really don't think at the time that's what we were doing. There are a few lines there that you think have to be about her, but I don't remember consciously writing about her.' Mel C similarly regarded the song as a more general reflection on how endings are a painful but unavoidable part of life to which everyone can relate, whether it's parting with a lover, a friend, or a family member. At its core 'Goodbye' is about the moments that slip out of grasp as time marches on. These reflections were pertinent for the Spice Girls after fame transformed their lives beyond recognition in the span of a few short years. 'Goodbye' bade farewell to the innocence of girlhood, to the comfort and security of living with family, to their anonymity as a band and as individuals, to Geri, and to the version of the Spice Girls that had once existed. 'I think what it's really about is saying goodbye to the naivety and pure joy we had writing the first two albums,' Biff concluded in a 2008 *Don't Stop The Pop* interview. Although Biff and Matt were unaware while working with the group in Nashville, half of the Spice Girls were pregnant and the joys, and contrasting obligations, of motherhood loomed for Mel B and Victoria. The track marks the end of a time free of adult responsibility. Like 'Viva Forever' before it, 'Goodbye' is imbued with an emotional heaviness that reflects the gruelling transition from girlhood to womanhood.

The Spice Girls, however, were not a group that dwelled on the negative. 'Look for the rainbow in every storm,' Mel B sings in the bridge, an uplifting nudge towards better days. And the group was right to be optimistic about the future—their stirring ballad made waves upon its 14 December 1998 debut when it became their third consecutive Christmas No. 1, a feat only previously achieved by The Beatles. It was a significant achievement that was even more meaningful given the tumult that had preceded it. Many critics interpreted Geri's departure as the final nail in the girl group's coffin but with 'Goodbye' they proved they had the stamina to endure as a four-piece. While detractors bet against them (both literally and figuratively, with the bookie William Hill reportedly losing over £250,000 on holiday chart bets between 1996 and 1998), the Spice Girls repeatedly defied the odds and kept clawing their way to No. 1. Although it had been a difficult year for the Spice Girls, they ended it on a high as the best-selling global act of 1998.

'It is a very sentimental song, and the first time I heard it I cried,' Mel B told *MTV News*. 'That was the first time I've cried listening to one of our songs, the first time I instantly cried. It's got a full orchestra on there and it just sounds fantastic.' As the first track to feature only four voices instead of five, 'Goodbye' cleverly accentuates the best of each girl's vocal abilities. Emma's childlike purity is tinged with sadness throughout the verses and is balanced by Mel B's husky tones in the bridge. Likewise, Victoria's contribution in the middle-8 is reflective and soulful and Mel C closes the song with vocals that perfectly balance pain and understanding as she pledges her support to her departed friend. 'You know it's time to say goodbye / And don't forget on me, you can rely / I will help you, help you on your way / I will be with you everyday.' Nearly two years after it climbed the charts as a single, 'Goodbye' was included as the closing track on the band's third album, *Forever*.

The song's accompanying music video was filmed at Mentmore Towers in Buckinghamshire over the course of two nights on 1 and 2 November 1998. The opulent mansion was constructed for the prominent Rothschild family in 1854 on a palatial property spanning 460,000 square feet and featured high ceilings and gilded walls. This château would serve as the spectacular backdrop for 'Goodbye', a video that translated the anguish of loss into a cinematic companion piece. The Spice Girls, bundled in thick winter coats, emerge from their respective vehicles and enter the imposing castle where they find an unsettling scene. All the occupants are frozen solid. Couples embracing, a woman taking a bath, a pair dancing—they are all rendered immobile, their complexions icy, their lips blue, and the frost in their eyelashes twinkling in the light. The video resolves when a thaw stretches through the mansion to wake inhabitants from their frigid slumbers. In an interview with *90s Noise*, director Howard Greenhalgh interpreted the video's concept as a depiction of the paralysis that followed Geri's abrupt resignation. Her departure momentarily stunned the world, and her bandmates, into stillness. With time the warmth returned, a reminder that while joy is fleeting, so is pain. Life resumed. And the Spice Girls survived.

Even though the band was able to move forward, Geri's exit remained a pain point for the band who felt it fundamentally altered their group identity. 'It was never the same when she left,' Victoria lamented in 2007. 'And other members might say oh it's great, we can do more complicated dance moves, we can sing more, it's like… that's not what we were about. We were about a vibe. We were about five girls.' On 15 June 2019, during the final night of the Spice World 2019 Tour, Geri prefaced the group's performance of 'Goodbye' at Wembley Stadium with a heartfelt speech. 'I need to say something very, very important that I should have said a long time ago—to Emma, to Melanie, to Melanie, and to the fans. I'm sorry. I'm sorry I left.' The four women blinked back tears and embraced as the crowd cheered. 'We say goodbye to the bad times and let's move on together,' she concluded before the quintet launched into the ballad, a moving moment only diminished by the fact that there were still only four women on stage. Yet again, a fifth was missing.

## 'CHRISTMAS WRAPPING'
Duration: 4:14
Written by Christopher Butler
Produced by Matt Rowe & Richard Stannard
Recording engineer: Adrian Bushby
Additional engineering by Jake Davies
Mixed by Jeremy Wheatley
Additional programming by Julian Gallagher
Saxophone by Richie Buckley
Trombone by Karl Ronan
Trumpet by Stephen McDonnell
Released as a B-side with 'Goodbye' on 14 December 1998

As a B-Side to their third and final Christmas No. 1, the Spice Girls recorded a cover of the 1981 holiday classic 'Christmas Wrapping' by American new wave group The Waitresses. It was first penned in an oppressive summer heat by the band's founding member, Chris Butler, after their label requested an original song for a Christmas compilation album. 'I was probably the least likely person to write a Christmas song,' Chris later remarked to the *Akron Beacon Journal*. 'I was a Scrooge. Christmas had always been a pain in the ass for me, frankly.' The song's title was a pun on a track called 'Christmas Rappin' that was released in 1979 by American rapper Kurtis Blow.

The original song tells the tale of a woman, voiced by lead singer Patty Donahue, who is exhausted after a whirlwind year and vows to skip Christmas and take it easy instead. 'Merry Christmas! But I think I'll miss this one this year,' she declares in the song's chorus. In the ensuing recap of her year, there is one recurring character, a man she fancies but can never connect with due to a series of unfortunate events. The narrative concludes when they cross paths in the grocery store and, finally in sync with each other, her icy heart is melted. In the chorus she shifts to a more positive outlook. 'Merry Christmas! Couldn't miss this one this year!' The Spice Girls' version follows the narrative of the original while incorporating some references to their own crazy year.

'Last year, world tour, aeroplanes and babies / We met some guys but never the time, most of '98 passed along those lines', Mel C sings in the opening verse. References to American grocery chain A&P are ditched in exchange for Tesco, a grocery store becomes a garage instead, and rather than shopping for cranberries, they're on the hunt for potatoes. 'It was slicker, dancier, and more polished than the original, sounding less like the new wave of 1981 and more like, well, the Spice Girls,' wrote Patrick Garvin for *The Pop Culture Experiment*.

As 1998 wound down, Spice-related work had to be redistributed to allow for half of the band to take some time off. 'With Mel B and Victoria both heavily pregnant as the year ended [...] Emma and I did the remaining promo,' Mel C detailed. In addition to chat show appearances and some international travel, this also included recording vocals for 'Christmas Wrapping'—the track only features performances by Mel C and Emma.

### 'SISTERS (ARE DOIN' IT FOR THEMSELVES)(LIVE)'
Duration: 4:20
Written by Annie Lennox & Dave Stewart
Recorded by Mike Dolling & Toby Alington
Mixed by Andy Bradfield
Released as a B-side with 'Goodbye' on 14 December 1998

The original version of 'Sisters Are Doin' It For Themselves' was written in 1985 by Annie Lennox and Dave Stewart of the Eurythmics. Inspired by the suffragette movement of the early 1900s that crusaded for a woman's right to vote, the duo decided to write an anthem celebrating female liberation. The track is an empowering ode to the mighty women who shattered the glass ceiling professionally to assume positions as doctors, lawyers, and politicians, roles previously out of reach for women relegated to the kitchen. Due to the subject matter, Annie Lennox wanted to feature another female performer on the track and after a crazy idea, a phone call, and a flight to Detroit, Michigan, they were recording with the Queen of Soul herself, Aretha Franklin. This was not Aretha's first feminist statement as decades earlier she had released an impactful gender-flipped take on Otis Redding's 'Respect'.

The Spice Girls rendition of the song features only Mel B and Mel C and was performed at all their 1998 tour dates. 'I love doing the duet with Mel C,' Mel B said of the number in *Forever Spice*. 'It's brilliant and vibey and it really gets the adrenaline going. You can really go for it visually, too, because although it's vocally set, the dance isn't a set routine, so we just run about being nutters on the stage.' Mel C also enjoyed the physicality of their performance. 'We could just jump around and be nutters,' she said of the track. 'I've not got good elevation, but I was always trying to jump as high as Damon from Blur.' The two Melanies also performed the cover on Channel 4's *TFI Friday* on 1 May 1998. The song's subject matter aligned with the Spice Girl's strong Girl Power messaging, making it a welcome addition to the setlist. 'When the group launched into a spirited take on the Annie Lennox–Aretha Franklin duet "Sisters Are Doin' It for Themselves," you could see the mothers in the crowd jump up in appreciation,' wrote Gilbert Garcia in a review of the band's tour stop in Phoenix, Arizona. The track seemed to be a favourite of the group both on and off stage—Mel C revealed in an April 1999 interview with *OK!* Magazine that she and Mel B had spontaneously burst into a performance of the song at a recent party hosted by her mother.

The Spice Girls' rendition of 'Sisters (Are Doin' It for Themselves)' was recorded during the final sold-out concert on the band's 1998 Spiceworld Tour at London's Wembley Stadium on 20 September 1998. The band allegedly recorded a studio version of the track in 1998, but it was shelved after Geri left.


## 'WE ARE FAMILY (LIVE)'
Duration: 3:35
Written by Bernard Edwards & Nile Rodgers
Recorded by Mike Dolling & Toby Alington
Mixed by Andy Bradfield
Released as a B-side with 'Goodbye' on 14 December 1998

'We Are Family' has been a staple of the Spice Girls' live concert experience for as long as they've been a touring act, and on their inaugural tour in 1998, it was featured prominently as their climactic closing number. 'We are family, I got all my sisters with me,' the five women sang in unison during the chorus, joyfully jumping to the beat of the music with their arms wrapped around one another. The band debuted the track during their very first tour stop on 24 February 1998. 'The Spice Girls silenced their critics when they kicked off their world tour with a dazzling Dublin performance,' claimed the *Belfast Telegraph* in a review that went on to praise their selection of 'We Are Family' as the closing number as 'perfect'.

In 1979, Nile Rodgers and Bernard Edwards of the Big Apple Band wrote the song 'We Are Family' for Sister Sledge, a disco soul group consisting of four siblings: Debbie, Joni, Kim, and Kathy Sledge. The song topped the charts and still regularly tops rankings of the most influential disco songs, dance songs, girl group songs and even the best pop songs of all time. While the Spice Girls didn't share blood as literally as the members of Sister Sledge, their group identity was so fundamentally built on the concept of sisterhood that the song's inclusion was a natural fit. For this reason, there was an added sting when the song remained on the setlist after Geri's May 1998 resignation—it was hard to shake the nagging feeling that a key member of the family was missing.

The live version released on the *Goodbye* EP was recorded during the final tour stop at London's Wembley Stadium on 20 September 1998. Just as with 'Sisters (Are Doin' It For Themselves)' it is believed that a studio version featuring Geri was recorded but was never released due to her unceremonious exit.

# Non-Album Tracks 1999

'My Strongest Suit'
Duration: 4:11
Composed by Elton John
Lyrics by Tim Rice
Produced by Richard Stannard, Matt Rowe & Phil Ramone
Mixed by Andy Bradfield
Electronic editing by Pat Thrall
Engineered by Adrian Bushby
Assisted by Pete Karam
Production managed by Jill Dell'Abate
Keyboards and programming by Matt Rowe
Additional programming by Jake Davies and Paul Waller
Additional recording and mixing by Frank Filipetti
Bass by Toby Baker
Additional bass by Zev Katz
Drums by Shawn Pelton
Guitar by Clem Clempson
Additional guitar and keyboards by Rob Mathes
Guitar and programming by Julian Gallagher
Tenor saxophone by Andy Snitzer
Trombone by Michael Davis
Trumpet by Jeff Kievit
Released on 23 March 1999 on *Elton John and Tim Rice's Aida*

The Spice Girls recorded 'My Strongest Suit' for *Elton John and Tim Rice's Aida*, a concept album that featured music from the forthcoming

Broadway musical, *Aida*. It was released a full year before the production had its theatrical debut and featured a litany of popular vocalists of the era, including Tina Turner, Sting, Janet Jackson, Shania Twain, and James Taylor. Based on the 1871 opera of the same name by writer Antonio Ghislanzoni and composer Giuseppe Verdi, the Broadway reimaging tells the story of an enslaved Nubian princess who falls in love with the Captain of the Egyptian army. In 1994, Disney acquired the story rights and intended to produce an animated feature film. Noted music and lyrics team Elton John and Tim Rice, however, had just experienced overwhelming critical and commercial success with *The Lion King* and were hesitant to retread the same territory with another animated film. When Disney executives proposed a Broadway adaption as a creative compromise, the pair immediately committed to the project.

In the musical stage production, 'My Strongest Suit' is performed in a palace spa by the Princess of Egypt, Amneris, who uses her keen sense of fashion as an armour to hide her vulnerabilities. 'So forget the inner me, observe the outer,' Amneris proclaims right before the song's beat kicks in. 'I am what I wear and how I dress.' As the number progresses, the spa transforms into a fashion show, with Women of the Palace modelling garments worthy of the catwalk. The track's subject matter was especially applicable to Victoria, a budding fashionista and future luxury fashion designer. Fashion would soon overtake performing as Victoria's primary form of self-expression. 'I had a lot of fun with the Spice Girls, but I don't miss those days and I don't miss being on stage. Fashion is where I feel comfortable, and where I feel excited,' she told *The Guardian* in 2020. 'I love making women feel like the best version of themselves.'

Elton John was already well-acquainted with the Spice Girls when he involved them in *Aida*—he made a cameo appearance in *Spice World The Movie*, performed his 1976 hit 'Don't Go Breaking My Heart' with the group during *An Audience With Elton John*, and had even developed close personal friendships with some of the girls, particularly Victoria and her husband David. 'I've always loved all the Disney films and I love *The Lion King*, so when Elton asked us about this, it was a huge honour,' Victoria said of the experience. The band's involvement in the early *Aida* recordings would have a ripple effect on the Broadway staging. When theatre designer Robert Crowley began listening to the concept album for design inspiration he watched as his 8-year-old niece became activated by the Spice Girls' rendition of 'My Strongest Suit'. She wiggled her way around the living room while singing along to the lyrics, yanking throw blankets from the furniture and wrapping them around her body as she strutted about, modelling her fashionable new look in a way that captured the spirit of the number. The song was subsequently played on loop. 'She drove us all crazy,' Robert told Patrick Pacheco of the *Los Angeles Times* in a December 1999 interview. But he used his niece's impassioned reaction to the song to inform his design decisions for the production.

Released on 23 March 1999, *Elton John and Tim Rice's Aida* sold only 170,000 copies between March and December of 1997 which had some sceptics fearing for the fate of the musical however the production was a financial success, was performed 1,852 times before closing in September 2004, and collected four Tony Awards during its run.

### 'IT'S ONLY ROCK 'N ROLL (BUT I LIKE IT)'
Duration: 4:49
Written by Mick Jagger & Keith Richards
Executive Produced by Lorna Dickinson & Mike Ingham
Produced and arranged by Arthur Baker
Mixed and programmed by Merv de Peyer
Released as a single by Artists for Children's Promise on 9 December 1999

At the close of the decade, a cover of the Rolling Stones' 1974 song 'It's Only Rock 'n Roll (But I Like It)' was produced to raise funds for Children's Promise, a union of non-profit organizations in the UK with a common goal of lifting children out of abuse, neglect, and poverty. The campaign, titled the Millennium Final Hour Appeal, urged the public to donate their last hour of pay from that calendar year to a worthy cause. Operating as a supergroup called Artists for Children's Promise, the Spice Girls were just one of many A-list participants. The track includes performances by Mick Jagger, Keith Richards, Annie Lennox, Chrissie Hynde, Dolores O'Riordan, Iggy Pop, Jon Bon Jovi, Kid Rock, Mary J. Blige, Ozzy Osbourne, and S Club 7 amongst countless others. In addition to a lengthy list of musical contributors, the track also featured famed comedians Eric Idle and Robin Williams. 'Children are our future and the great range of artists who have taken part in the Children's Promise "Rock 'N' Roll" charity record is a testimony to the universal importance of a safe and secure childhood,' read the liner notes of the single. 'This record aims to promote the aims of Children's Promise while celebrating the music that has changed this century.'

The featured artists recorded their parts individually over the span of several months when their busy schedules permitted, with the Spice Girls completing their vocals at London's Whitfield Street Studios in the summer of 1999 while hard at work on *Forever*. Though the Rolling Stones had not initially intended to perform on the track, Mick Jagger and Keith Richards decided to use their star power to boost the track's charitable message. This desire to reach as many people as possible is likely why the Spice Girls were at the very top of producers' wishlists. The girl group's impressive album sales and youth appeal would attract a very different demographic than a featured artist like Ozzy Osbourne. The Spice Girls are featured prominently on the track (even being introduced by name) and in the accompanying music video where artists are shown recording their vocal segments in studio.

Despite being released in the lead up to the holidays in a bid for a Christmas No. 1, the track debuted at No. 19 on the UK charts, losing handily to Westlife who snagged the last No. 1 of the '90s, and the millennium, with the double A-side release of 'Seasons in the Sun'/'I Have a Dream'.

# 7

# *Forever*

The Spice Girls released their third and final studio album on 6 November 2000. It yielded one double A-side single which reached No. 1 in the UK and entered the top 10 in over a dozen countries. The album peaked at No. 2 upon release and has since been certified Platinum. *Forever* has sold over two million copies worldwide.

### 'Holler'
Duration: 4:15
Written by Rodney Jerkins, LaShawn Daniels, Fred Jerkins III, Victoria Beckham, Melanie Brown, Emma Bunton & Melanie Chisholm
Produced by Rodney Jerkins
Vocal Production by LaShawn 'The Big Shiz' Daniels
Protocols by Harvey Mason Jr
Recorded by Brad Gilderman
Assisted by Dave Russell & Ian Robertson
Mixed by Brad Gilderman & Rodney Jerkins
Released as a single 23 October 2000

From the opening notes of 'Holler' it is abundantly clear that a new era of Spice has begun. The sexually charged dance track opens with a distorted male voice murmuring over computerised guitar strums: 'Spice Girls. Darkchild. 2000.' It's the first time that a man is featured on any Spice Girls track and after nearly two years of waiting for a new single from the girl group it's a somewhat jarring reintroduction.

The unfamiliar voice belongs to Rodney Jerkins, a writer-producer better known by his stage name Darkchild, who began making waves in the American pop scene during the 1990s with his twist on contemporary R&B. At 17, the wunderkind signed a publishing deal with EMI Records worth $1.8 million, from which he produced a series of critical and commercial home runs. Star-making singles such as 'If You Had My Love' by Jennifer Lopez, 'Say My Name' by Destiny's Child, and Brandy and Monica's 'The Boy Is Mine', all written and produced under his creative counsel, established him as a rising star with a keen insight into the future of the genre. A-list musicians clamoured for the opportunity to work with him and by the time he was working with the Spice Girls, he already had projects with Michael Jackson and Britney Spears in the pipeline. Rodney was much more than an anonymous figure lurking in the background of a popstar's production—he had a recognisable sound and style and his name carried weight. This brand identity inspired the development of a sonic signature, the word 'Darkchild' woven into his tracks as a sort of audio calling card.

The Spice Girls began work on their third album in the autumn of 1998 but as writing progressed their musical sensibilities shifted. They gravitated away from the brazen pop sound that frequent collaborators Biff Stannard, Matt Rowe and Eliot Kennedy had helped them craft and moved towards a more sophisticated and soulful R&B sound. This curiosity was encouraged by their long-time A&R representative at Virgin Records, Ashley Newton, who had recently relocated from London to Los Angeles. His increased exposure to American trends had him thinking about how a stylistic progression could benefit the English girl group and give them a stronger foothold in the United States. Emma and Mel C, who were still carrying the bulk of Spice-related duties while Victoria and Mel B were on maternity leave, met Rodney Jerkins for dinner in New York and expressed their interest in working with him. It was reciprocated by Rodney and sessions were booked. He pledged to bring an 'urban, danceable' quality to the Spice Girls' third album. 'It will still have a pop appeal, but the beats will be a little harder,' he told *MTV News* after rumours of the collaboration surfaced. The girl group was hopeful that Rodney's credibility would transfer to their group, ushering them into an esteemed class of pop. They began sessions with Rodney on 25 August 1999 at Whitfield Street Studios in London. 'This is more American sounding for us but then I think that's the way that pop music is going,' Victoria reasoned upon the single's release. As they saw it, they were simply adapting with the times.

Rodney ran a wholesome, family operation—aided by his older brother Fred Jerkins III and long-time family friend LaShawn Daniels, he developed a dependable songwriting assembly line. Rodney would first experiment with a drum machine and keyboard until a worthy foundation emerged. The bones of a new song would then be passed along to Fred and LaShawn, who added lyrics and a melody line. It was this process that birthed 'Holler', and while the Spice Girls had input, they were more hands-off than they had been for *Spice* or *Spiceworld*. 'I think [we were involved] less on this album,' Mel C reflected during an interview at Inflight Studios. 'With Rodney he's such a fantastic producer and... the songs are our babies, but the production is his. If there was something we didn't like, it'd be changed but really, you'd have to go off and let him work and do his magic.'

The son of a reverend, Rodney's Pentecostal roots impacted the way he ran his workspace. Smoking, drinking, drug use, and swearing were all prohibited in his studio, something it was hard for visitors to forget due to the framed warning signs that decorated the space. But even with the reminders the Darkchild crew still had to correct one bad habit of the Spice Girls. 'They used bad language a little bit, here and there,' Fred revealed in David Sinclair's *Wannabe: How The Spice Girls Reinvented Pop*. 'But if they did, they would usually catch themselves—'Ooops! We're not supposed to do that because the Jerkins boys are here'—and laugh about it.' The puritanical climate in the studio certainly did not extend to the track's subject matter which presents a more lascivious version of the Spice Girls than seen previously. Mel B leads the first verse with a tempting invitation to her fantasy room, Victoria croons about getting her man to do things he thought he'd never do, Mel C promises to be someone's all-night fantasy, and Emma sheds the last remnants of her virginal image when she sings, 'You gotta show me boy 'cause nothing comes for free / Start from the bottom and work your way up slowly'. It weaves a more adult narrative, trading in the suggestive remarks and innuendos from their early works for explicitly sexual propositions. It's also a departure from the female-first mindset that had become their trademark—while the female protagonists are the dominant parties, the ultimate goal appears to be male pleasure. The Spice Girls set the rules for their partners but it's the men who are rewarded for complying.

Behind the scenes, the group knew that a smooth rollout of *Forever* was essential after such a lengthy absence and feared that a misstep with the first single could jeopardize the album's commercial performance. 'I'll never forget making the phone call to Emma saying, 'Emma come on, what do you think, it's down to you,' Mel B recounted. 'The first song that we're going to release is going to get scrutinised, loved, hated, whatever. So we had to be 100%. And if anything goes wrong, we'll just blame it on Emma,' she concluded with a playful laugh. The band had already begun building anticipation for 'Holler' on the 1999 Christmas in Spiceworld Tour and had performed it at the BRITs in March 2000 when they were honoured with an award for Outstanding Contribution to Music so they took advantage of this pre-existing public awareness.

The Spice Girls filmed the music video for 'Holler' on 27 and 28 July 2000 in London's Elstree Studios with new styles to match their new sound. Their leather-and-chains accoutrement was paired with smoky makeup and new edgier hairstyles; Mel C was blonde, Emma had blunt bangs, Victoria's signature bob was history and her waist-length tresses whipped around wildly in the wind. During scenes in which Mel B writhed sexily on a bed in lingerie her hair was piled in a long, braided ponytail. When asked if the stylistic changes were indicative of a concerted image overhaul for the band Emma denied that the Spice Girls were distancing themselves from their kid-friendly personas. 'Not at all, I think that was just really a natural progression. We've all kind of just grown up,' she stressed. 'It wasn't like we all went right, we're going to put leather on and look older. It didn't work like that. The whole leather look came because the video was futuristic and quite hard.' Directed by Jake Nava, the video was a CGI-heavy foray set in a crystal pyramid. The girls performed their respective verses solo, accompanied only by the male models that they hand selected for themselves. Each girl represents one of the four elements in her themed room: Mel B is fire, Mel C is earth, Emma is water, and Victoria is air. At the core of the pyramid the four Spice Girls reunite to gyrate and execute their synchronised group choreography, their backs turned to one another. There is a feeling of disconnectedness in their positioning and their body language is not that of a unified band but rather of four individuals occupying the same space, possibly a sign that transitioning back into a girl group after working solo wasn't as effortless as they suggested. 'When you're off doing your solo bits, it's lovely but it's nothing like having your girlies about,' Emma said, dismissing the idea that working alone was preferable.

'Holler' was released on 23 October 2000 with ballad 'Let Love Lead the Way' in a double A-side single and despite scepticism from critics about the band's lasting power in the new millennium sales were strong. The day after the single dropped, HMV's head of press, Gennaro Castaldo, spoke to BBC News about the public's continued support for the girl group. 'It's picked up very strongly and has been quite an underground hit and could pose a challenge if sales pick up again with more stock in the shops,' he said. 'Although we may not still have the days of Spice mania, the girls are still a very powerful group and the whole is greater than the sum of the parts. They still have that old magic.' Selling 106,000 copies in the first week, 'Holler' debuted at No. 1, becoming the group's ninth and final single to top the charts. The Spice Girls remain the only girl group to achieve nine No. 1s in the UK—their closest competition to date has been Little Mix who snagged five No. 1s between 2011 and 2021.

Craig Seymour of *R&Being* applauded this smoother, groovier version of the band. 'On their new single, "Holler," the Ginger-less Spice Girls sound like they really, really wanna be Destiny's Child,' he wrote. 'And while they'll win no points for originality, the tune has its charms: an easy yet funky groove, their exaggerated British […] and Jerkins' familiar slapping, kinetic beats. Their most compelling reason to dance since "Say You'll Be There."' Some, however, felt that the negatives outweighed the positives. David Browne of *Entertainment Weekly* noted that the vocal performances had 'little spunk or energy', suggesting that the dedication of some band members had faded. Others found it to be a mismatch of creative minds. While no individual piece of the puzzle was necessarily at fault, for many the R&B sound just didn't suit the Spice Girls as well as it suited artists like Usher and Mariah Carey. The first two Spice Girls albums were collections of pastiches in an array of retro styles which allowed the Spice Girls to exist outside of current trends but because 'Holler' was produced to sound so quintessentially 2000s it is also a more dated chapter of the band's career.

On 16 November 2000, the Spice Girls travelled to Stockholm, Sweden to perform their latest No. 1 hit at the MTV European Music Awards—this performance of 'Holler' would be their last public appearance as a group until their 2007 reunion.

## 'Tell Me Why'

Duration: 4:14
Written by Rodney Jerkins, Fred Jerkins III, LaShawn Daniels, Mischke Butler, Victoria Beckham, Melanie Brown & Emma Bunton
Produced by Rodney Jerkins
All music by Rodney Jerkins
Vocal production by LaShawn 'The Big Shiz' Daniels
Recorded by Paul Foley
Mixed by Ben Garrison & Rodney Jerkins

Before *Forever*, the Spice Girls shared songwriting credit evenly on all their work, a decision that set the standard for many future pop acts. The band understood that their strength was their unity and decided to structure their credits, and their royalties, accordingly. For their first two albums they without fail adhered to a rigid five-way split regardless of who contributed which ideas to which song, knowing that it all balanced out in the bigger picture. 'Tell Me Why' is the first Spice Girls track that fails to credit all current band members and with hindsight the dissolution of their collective arrangement was an early sign that the wheels were coming off the Spice Bus.

'Tell Me Why' was written in April 2000 when the Spice Girls travelled to Miami, Florida to continue working on new material with the Darkchild team. Virgin was pleased with the results of their first sessions together in 1999 and were encouraging the group to further explore this new R&B influenced pop sound. But upon arriving in Miami a bombshell was dropped on the band—not all of the Spice Girls would be in attendance. 'When we got there, we found out that Mel C wasn't coming but would be putting down her vocals later,' Victoria recalled in her memoir *Learning To Fly*. 'At first, we thought it was just that her schedule clashed, but it wasn't long before we realised that there was more to it.'

Mel C was struggling. She had gone directly from the 1998 Spiceworld Tour, straight into the studio to work on her debut solo album, *Northern Star*, and then immediately back on the road to promote her new album without ever taking a moment to collect herself. Her mental health was deteriorating, she was depressed, and her eating disorder was out of control, oscillating between strict food restriction with obsessive exercise and binge eating. Every pound gained or lost was dissected in tabloids where she was nicknamed Beefy Spice and Sumo Spice. She couldn't handle the idea of returning to the studio with the Spice Girls. 'I was ill at that time, so I suppose I just didn't have the strength to deal with it to be honest with you,' she later reflected. She felt as though the band had reached a natural conclusion; Geri was gone, Mel B and Victoria had started families, and every band member was looking ahead to the future and strategising about solo careers. She was ready to go in a new direction. 'I [...] didn't want to do *Forever* at all, whatsoever,' Mel C bemoaned in her memoir. 'Not then, not at that point. I wanted to finish up *Northern Star*, take a break and then think about the future of the Spice Girls and my place within it.' But the other girls felt differently.

'At the end of the day I think being a Spice Girl is a bit like a marriage,' Victoria mused in her autobiography. 'Compromise is a central part of it. You get the "for better" and the "for worse."' But during this period, Mel C had lost her willingness to compromise. She'd experienced success as a solo artist and was no longer motivated to find a middle ground. As she wrestled with a distorted sense of self, the thought of shedding the baggage of being a Spice Girl was appealing. 'It had been two years since the end of the American tour and we had all grown up, but Mel C had also grown away—not least in terms of her music,' Victoria reflected. 'She was always more rock 'n' roll than the rest of us, but that was what she brought to the group.' Now she was being forced to pore over R&B tracks. 'The feeling of being in an environment that I didn't want to be in began to grow,' Mel C reflected. She recorded many of her vocal parts separately, withdrew socially from the group, and minimised her creative contributions. And yet, even with her involvement waning, she felt she couldn't leave and bear the responsibility for the end of the Spice Girls. 'I felt completely trapped,' she wrote in her memoir. 'If it was me who ended the Spice Girls, I would be so hated. I was too scared about the backlash from the media. I feared hurting the fans. I feared the girls. I was trapped. I didn't know where to go. I didn't know what to do.'

Victoria, Mel B and Emma soldiered on, their quintet having now dwindled down to a trio. With creative guidance from Darkchild, the three of them wrote about what they knew best at that time: fractured friendships. Long-time fans raised their eyebrows upon a closer reading of the 'Tell Me Why' lyrics. 'We started with dreams / We started a team / [...] Yet you turned your back and walked out on me.' Although it had now been a couple years since Geri's walkout it was still a sticking point with fans and, many surmised, with the remaining four Spice Girls as well. When asked directly by *The Guardian* in 2019 if the track was about Geri, Emma tried to remain diplomatic, but her silence spoke volumes. 'I think at that time, yeah, when we were writing songs we were being very honest and open, which I think is great.' She averted her glance and began distractedly smoothing her skirt. 'Er... and... yeah, we were writing how we felt at that point.' Later in the track when Mel B croons, 'You're the one who decided to erase all our plans', it's hard to imagine that the subject matter could be anyone other than their redheaded ex-bandmate.

James Hunter for *Rolling Stone* described the track as having a 'silky, spiky danceability'. These qualities are likely why the band contemplated releasing it as a single, however, plans were shelved when *Forever* failed to live up to sales expectations set by the band's prior two staggeringly successful albums.

## 'LET LOVE LEAD THE WAY'
Duration: 4:58
Written by Rodney Jerkins, LaShawn Daniels, Fred Jerkins III, Harvey Mason Jr, Victoria Beckham, Melanie Brown, Emma Bunton & Melanie Chisholm
Produced by Harvey Mason Jr & Rodney Jerkins
All music by Harvey Mason Jr & Rodney Jerkins
Vocal production by LaShawn 'The Big Shiz' Daniels
Protocols by Harvey Mason Jr
Recorded by Brad Gilderman
Assisted by Dave Russell & Ian Robertson
Mixed by Rodney Jerkins & Brad Gilderman
Released as a single on 23 October 2000

'Let Love Lead the Way' is an existential R&B ballad in which the Spice Girls, a group once dismissed as creators of meaningless confection, wrestle with the juxtaposition of joy and pain and the disillusionment that accompanies the shattering of a child's rosy worldview. 'You switch on the TV and you see all the death and destruction on the news and just think, "Why? Why is the world like this?"' Mel C said, elaborating on the song's subject matter. 'When you're very young, you're innocent and naïve. And when you start finding out all the horrible things about the world, it just really lets you down, doesn't it?' Despite the song's gloomy impetus, the underlying message is one of hope and optimism—for every dark or cruel act there is kindness to counterbalance. 'Even though there's horrible things going on outside in the world […] you have to let love take you where you want to go; believe in yourself, trust yourself and wash the other horrible things away,' Emma articulated. During earlier versions of the track, the song's protagonist was an unhoused individual enduring extreme hardship, but this was later revised to be a young girl who acts as an audience surrogate.

The music video for 'Let Love Lead the Way' started filming in London on 17 July 2000 and is a conceptual companion to the music video for 'Holler'. Once again, the Spice Girls each embody one of the four classical elements from Greek philosophy. This time around Mel B personifies the element of air, sporting crisp white clothing in a space framed with fluttering ivory fabric walls. The atmosphere is light and breezy and feathers drift by weightlessly. Dressed in a silky forest green dress, Emma portrays the element of earth. She sings serenely while lying in the grass at the base of a gnarled oak tree and resembles a woodland nymph with her long wavy golden locks spread around her. Victoria is fire, styled in a slinky crimson dress in a scorched wasteland consumed by darkness, flames licking the dried desert plants behind her. And finally, Mel C, dressed in a tie-dyed tank top and blue trousers, embodies water. She performs next to a calm pool before submitting to the shower of the surrounding waterfalls. 'Even though we are different elements and we are different people, when we come together it just goes right into place,' Emma said of how the elemental concept connected to their band identity. This is emphasised in the video's narrative when the girls come together as a unit in the song's chorus and their chemistry sparks on screen.

The Spice Girls appreciated director Gregg Masuak's efficiency on set. He was quick to establish a relaxed atmosphere and workdays were relatively short, a pleasant contrast to the upcoming shoot for 'Holler' which dragged late into the night and well into the next morning. Prolonged shoots had plagued the band since their early days with lengthy tear-down and set-up periods required for each girl's individual segments. While one girl filmed her parts the others were stuck killing time until it was their turn. 'You just sit and eat all day,' Victoria said of how dull shooting days could be. But the two-day shoot for 'Let Love Lead the Way' was an enjoyable one. Victoria's trailer ended up doubling as a nursery where her son and Mel B's daughter, both a few months shy of their second birthdays, played and rested. 'It was all rather lovely,' Victoria reflected in her memoir. Only Mel C had a slightly unpleasant shoot—her waterfall scenes were filmed at the end of the second day and she was left drenched and shivering late into the evening as cameras were repositioned to get the necessary shots.

'"Let Love Lead the Way" is fantastic because it's a big, big ballad but it's funny because when we're actually taping it […] they do it double speed,' Victoria revealed. 'You sound like a chipmunk.' To get the desired dreamy effect, the girls needed to synchronise their performance with a sped-up version of the song. When the footage was slowed to match the song's actual speed, the visuals gained a dramatic slow-motion effect. 'You look very strange,' Victoria laughed during an MTV *Making the Video* featurette, noting that to achieve the right look she had to move her body unnaturally. Despite feeling silly during filming the finished result is ethereal and cinematic, a glossy video with vivid pops of colour and performances full of yearning. 'Everything will work out fine / If you let love, love lead the way', the quartet sings with conviction.

The track had its radio debut on 6 October 2000 and debuted at No. 1 following its formal double A-side release with 'Holler' on 23 October

2000. 'We've picked probably the most contrasting songs on the album,' Mel C said of the single selection process. '"Holler" is a good dance track and "Let Love Lead the Way" is a really good ballad.' The band hoped to showcase the album's range by pairing a sexy club bop with a soft and emotional number. While some critics praised the ballad as one of *Forever*'s shining moments, others criticised it as feeling restrained and generic.

'Right Back At Ya'
Duration: 4:11
Written by Victoria Beckham, Melanie Brown, Emma Bunton, Melanie Chisholm, Eliot Kennedy & Tim Lever
Produced by Uncle Freddie
All music by Fred Jerkins
Vocal production by LaShawn 'The Big Shiz' Daniels
Additional vocal production by Eliot Kennedy & Sue Drake
Backing vocals by Eliot Kennedy & Sue Drake
Recorded by Ben Garrison
Assisted by Dave Russell
Mixed by Ben Garrison & Fred Jerkins III

The Spice Girls gave fans a sneak peek of their upcoming third album when they debuted 'Right Back At Ya' on their 1999 Christmas in Spiceworld Tour. They performed it at all eight dates, clad in bright individualised monochromatic outfits, the thumping of the track's funky bassline whipping the sold-out arenas into a frenzy. The peppy tempo and whining melodic synth embellishments ensured the track fit seamlessly into the Spice catalogue.

'We just feel like since the first single [...] people have been saying, 'Oh it's the end of them, they're a one hit wonder, they're this, they're that,' Mel C said during the November 2000 press cycle for the release of *Forever*. 'We've had to deal with that all the way through our career. And here we are with our third album coming right back at ya.' The song challenges the group's detractors head on, with Mel C crooning, 'You thought we wouldn't make it this far, so we proved you wrong again' in the opening verse. It also pays homage to their roots when Emma sings that, 'real friendship never ends'. Mel B contributes one of her signature raps towards the song's close, asserting, 'They all try and diss us but there ain't nothing in it, we started a trend now they all imitated / A new generation of spice we created.' The song is a celebration of drive and perseverance, and also calls attention to their sprawling influence, something that has been proven in subsequent decades with the likes of Adele, Sam Smith, HAIM, Little Mix, and Dua Lipa all citing the Spice Girls as an early influence.

The Spice Girls wrote the song with Eliot Kennedy at Steelworks Studios during an August 1999 visit to Sheffield. Over the course of a week, they workshopped several promising tracks, and 'Right Back At Ya' quickly emerged as a favourite. 'It was one of the funkiest tracks I've ever done,' Eliot said in *Wannabe: How The Spice Girls Reinvented Pop*. 'The idea was to get a comeback record that would hit you right in your face. The girls were buzzing off it, the record company loved it.' Shortly after these sessions, however, the Spice Girls met with Rodney Jerkins and with his influence the album started to drift in a different direction. Suddenly the band's interest in their tracks with Eliot began to wane until nearly all had been cut from *Forever*. 'Right Back At Ya' was the only song on *Forever* written with a British collaborator aside from Matt Rowe and Biff Stannard's 'Goodbye' released in 1998 and included as the album's closing track. The remainder of the tracks were generated with their new American pals.

Even though the song survived the chopping block it underwent some major reworking before being added to *Forever* and cowriter Eliot Kennedy wasn't pleased with the results. The song had undergone an R&B transformation when it was rerecorded and remixed by Fred and Ben of the Darkchild team—gone was the funky bassline, the big pop sound, and rollicking beat from Eliot's version. The R&B version was less urgent, with a sparser arrangement and an electronic beat. It no longer struck the listener with force and Eliot was devastated when he heard the album mix. 'I was gutted,' he sighed. 'So much so that I really wish it hadn't gone on the album. I wish we'd saved it in its original form and done something else with it. They'd taken all the fun out of the song and reduced it to this plodding, boring, bottom drawer R&B song. This was such a bad call.' He felt this misstep was part of a larger miscalculation by Virgin about how the band could most effectively capture the American market. They were actively pursuing an 'American' sound but coming from a quartet of British women the results felt inauthentic. 'It was nothing to do with music that third album,' Eliot hypothesised. 'They wanted to try and max the sales as much as they could by making an American record for America. And they lost all their audience in the process.'

Spice Girls fans unexpectedly got a taste of Eliot's preferred version in February 2015 when four unreleased tracks were unceremoniously uploaded on SoundCloud, one of which was the pop mix of 'Right Back At Ya'. It aligned closely with the punchier pop version performed live by the group in 1999. The track disappeared from the audio-sharing platform as suddenly as it had materialised but the news made headlines and fans celebrated this unearthed Girl Power relic—this was several years into a Spice drought and any new material was savoured by those praying for the band's return. The more energetic mix was well-received by those who streamed the bootleg upload, perhaps vindicating Eliot Kennedy in the process.

## 'GET DOWN WITH ME'
Duration: 3:46
Written by Rodney Jerkins, LaShawn Daniels, Fred Jerkins III, Robert Smith, Mischke Butler, Victoria Beckham, Melanie Brown & Emma Bunton
Produced by Rodney Jerkins & Robert Smith
All music by Rodney Jerkins & Robert Smith
Vocal production by LaShawn 'The Big Shiz' Daniels
Recorded by Paul Foley
Mixed by Ben Garrison & Rodney Jerkins

'Get Down With Me' is *Forever*'s most boisterous R&B dance track– the tempo is upbeat and the electronic strings that lead the melody line are sharp and frisky, perfectly matching the tone of the aggressively flirtatious lyrics. It depicts a focused pursuit led by our Spice protagonists, who make promises about the night of fun they can provide a crush, embodied by Darkchild, who punctuates the girls' lines with interjections before the girls move on. 'Now that we have been together for a night it's time for you and I to say goodbye / Don't try to hold on to this moment because when you wake up I'll be gone', they sing in unison towards the song's close. The infatuation was extinguished as suddenly it had begun. The track and the affair alike are nothing more than a dose of fun ephemera.

Mischke Butler and Robert Smith are each credited writers on the track, both of whom were brought into the Darkchild collective under Rodney's wing to be mentored during this period. They would eventually go on to individually have successful songwriting and production careers of their own, with Mischke leaning into vocal coaching and arranging for artists including JoJo and Little Mix. Robert, better known as Big Bert, stayed in the production lane and built tracks for Toni Braxton and Kelly Rowland. While Rodney's packed stable of talent was busy generating ideas for *Forever* 'Get Down With Me' is missing input from a key member of the Spice team; Mel C is omitted from the writing credits due to her absence in the studio.

### 'Wasting My Time'
Duration: 4:14
Written by Fred Jerkins III, LaShawn Daniels, Melanie Brown, Emma Bunton & Melanie Chisholm
Produced by Uncle Freddie
All music by Fred Jerkins III
Vocal production by LaShawn 'The Big Shiz' Daniels
Recorded by Ben Garrison
Assisted by Dave Russell
Mixed by Ben Garrison & Fred Jerkins III

'You thought that you'd play me and have things your way, so can you blame me for walking away / What did I do to be treated so bad / Now you have lost me and I was the best thing you'd ever had', the Spice Girls sing in the first verse of 'Wasting My Time'. It's a breakup track that, despite its playful R&B bounce and synthesiser embellishments, pulls no punches. While the Spice Girls had all endured their fair share of hookups and breakups, the song was especially pertinent for one band member who very publicly met a new partner, hastily got engaged, fell pregnant, got married, and then filed for divorce, all in the time between the group's second and third albums.

Melanie Brown met Dutch dancer Jimmy Gulzar in February 1998, after he was cast as one of the male dancers, or Spice Boys, in the upcoming Spiceworld Tour. He bore a striking resemblance to her high school sweetheart which created a false sense of familiarity for Mel. 'It felt as if he was pulling me towards him with a rope,' she explained. Despite Mel's immediate attraction to Jimmy, it was not love at first sight. Jimmy was cold and distant, which confounded Mel who was accustomed to be the pursued, not the pursuer. This power dynamic, so unfamiliar to Mel, compelled her to work even harder to win Jim's affection. 'He really aroused my curiosity,' she recalled in her 2002 memoir *Catch A Fire*. 'His personality was a blank and he showed me nothing. That made me want to find out more about him, get under his skin. I *had* to.' Both Mel and Jim had partners when they met but with her attention fixed elsewhere, her relationship quickly fizzled. She only had capacity for Jim.

Eventually Mel's persistence paid off and Jimmy succumbed to her advances. 'I didn't care that he seemed quite awkward as he kissed me, didn't notice that he held my hips really stiffly, like an eight-year-old would, with rigid arms and hands,' she said. 'The only thing that mattered at the time was that something was finally happening between us.' They went on their first date while in Paris for the Spice Girls' performances at the Zénith de Paris on 22 and 23 March 1998. The couple had an extravagant dinner at the Buddha Bar, sat at glimmering mosaic tables with Indian music playing softly. Despite the romantic evening, things remained chaste between the pair. 'We didn't have sex together for a long time and, to be honest, I can't remember where or when the first time was,' she wrote in her memoir. 'It just didn't seem to matter to him whether he had sex or not. I couldn't understand it but I was intrigued—and determined to win him over.' On 13 May 1998, less than two months after their first date, Jimmy planned another dinner at the Buddha Bar and proposed. Mel ecstatically accepted. She'd spent all of her energy over the last few months trying to prove that she could win Jimmy over but had never paused to ask herself if she should.

In the end, the engagement just shone more light on the couple's issues. Mel had convinced herself that with time stressors would dissipate and their relationship would find its rhythm but their plans to wed did nothing to remedy their sexual dysfunctions. Money also became an issue with a concerned Mel C at one point begging a spend-happy Mel B to stop buying Jimmy so many expensive presents. These concerns were echoed by Mel B's family and when her mother urged the pair to sign a prenuptial agreement, Jimmy refused and a feud ensued. The financial concerns of Mel's friends and family were not in vain—Jimmy had already asked Mel for money to pay back personal debts. Messages of caution were also issued from complete strangers. On a night out at a club, one of Jimmy's ex-girlfriends approached Mel and whispered an ominous warning in her ear. 'Just... be careful, that's all.' Eventually Mel heeded the countless warnings and broke off the engagement but a couple days later Mel learned some shocking news—she was pregnant. This changed her outlook entirely. 'The pregnancy made everything all right again. I couldn't get back together with Jim fast enough,' Mel wrote about the experience. 'Suddenly everything had slotted into place. I wanted to be with him, I'd always wanted to have a baby and now I was pregnant with a miracle child. There was no escaping my destiny now, even though I knew in my heart that the relationship just wasn't right.' Mel and Jimmy tied the knot on 13 September 1998, at St. John the Baptist Church in Little Marlow, Buckinghamshire, in a splashy event that came with a £500,000 price tag. No detail was overlooked with silk tablecloths, a towering cake decorated with marzipan doves, and an abundance of white delphiniums, phlox, and lilies. The evening concluded with a £10,000 firework display.

Rumours swirled from the outset about tension in the relationship and the tabloid press didn't have to wait long before the saga reached an explosive conclusion while Jimmy and Mel were on vacation. What started as an attempt to salvage family unity, ended in a raging argument. 'Mel and Jimmy have confirmed that they are to separate,' the pair announced in a joint statement on 2 January 2000. 'The couple have arrived at this conclusion after a considerable amount of discussions and attempts to make the relationship work.' The split was messy, with Mel publicly discussing how Jimmy neglected her in bed and Jimmy, in turn, alleging that Mel had a breast augmentation, something he disapproved of as it prevented her from breastfeeding their newborn. There was also an altercation between Jimmy and Mel's sister where he allegedly seized her by the throat and spat in her face. He was found guilty of assault but later cleared due to evidentiary issues. Jimmy demanded £3 million to dissolve the marriage (of which he reportedly received a settlement of £700,000) and the divorce was finalised after five months. 'It was the most miserable time of my life, but I don't regret any of it,' Mel reflected. 'I've gained power from what I went through, because I've been able to understand myself more.'

The painful breakdown of Mel's marriage undoubtedly shaped the direction of 'Wasting My Time' where there exists a simmering anger that does not perforate the radio-friendly sound but is unmistakable in the song's lyrics. 'You should see that it's not all about you, this time you played too many games / Now it's time to see that I won't waste my life, no not me,' the Spice Girls sing. For Mel, doubling down on the mistake and staying in a toxic situation was not an option so in a move that exemplified the spirit of Girl Power she chose to put her happiness and well-being ahead of her pride. It ushered the band into a new era—gone are the schoolyard squabbles of young love and instead the Spice Girls are left grappling with the weightier disappointments of adult relationships.

'Weekend Love'
Duration: 4:06
Written by Rodney Jerkins, Fred Jerkins III, LaShawn Daniels, Victoria Beckham, Melanie Brown, Emma Bunton & Melanie Chisholm

Produced by Rodney Jerkins
All music by Rodney Jerkins
Vocal production by LaShawn 'The Big Shiz' Daniels
Protocols by Harvey Mason Jr
Recorded by Brad Gilderman
Assisted by Dave Russell & Ian Robertson
Mixed by Brad Gilderman & Rodney Jerkins

'["Weekend Love"] was something we all came up with,' Mel C recounted in a 2000 Inflight Studios interview. 'It's just putting the boot on the other foot really.' From the opening sitar strums, the ballad explores a casual fling that has naturally run its course—unfortunately the man in the equation is unaware that this wasn't something more. It's a subversion of the stereotype that expects women to be clingy while men are allowed to treat women as disposable. 'We thought no, this time we want to be the ones in control. The guy is gagging for it, and she's not interested,' Mel C elaborated. 'Weekend love—that's all he was. Move on. Pack your bags. Next one in.'

The lyrics speak directly to this former-flame and attempt to let him down easy. In the opening lines Emma sings, 'You thought that this was love / But my plan wasn't that for us / I thought that you would understand / I didn't want you for my full-time man'. The track coddles the man's emotions to a certain degree, even complimenting his sexual prowess, but as the track nears its close Mel B delivers a rap verse that infuses the song with some much-needed bite. 'Every time I turn around, you're standing right there, I really don't want you and I really don't care,' she spits. Mel B listed the song as one of her favourites on the album, likely a reason it was flagged as a potential single, but it wasn't to be. As the band ceased promotional efforts for *Forever*, 'Weekend Love' was left for only the diehard Spice Girls fans spinning the full album.

## 'TIME GOES BY'
Duration: 4:51
Written by Fred Jerkins III, Rodney Jerkins, LaShawn Daniels, Mischke Butler, Victoria Beckham, Melanie Brown & Emma Bunton
Produced by Rodney Jerkins & Uncle Freddie
All music by Fred Jerkins III & Rodney Jerkins
Vocal production by LaShawn 'The Big Shiz' Daniels
Recorded by Paul Foley
Mixed by Ben Garrison & Rodney Jerkins

'Time Goes By' is a classically romantic keyboard-driven ballad with emotional lyrics about undying love. 'Time goes by but we stand still / Love you for eternity I will / I know that we were meant to be / That's how I feel when you're with me,' the band harmonises during the chorus, their voices lush and sincere. '["Time Goes By"] is beautiful,' Emma said emphatically. 'We said let's do a ballad where we're in love! We're not going to tell him what to do, we're not going to say, "I'm in love with you BUT... don't push it",' she said laughing. 'So we just did a pure ballad and at the time I think we were all thinking about men in our lives.' Emma likely had Jade Jones on her mind while she crooned, a member of the boy band Damage with whom she first connected in 1998. 'Both of us knew we wanted to be together. We're soul mates. [But] it hit us that we were so young and both of us haven't done everything, we did have a break,' Emma reflected later during an appearance on Holly Willoughby's podcast *By the Light of the Moon*. 'It gave us time to grow as people and when we came back together, it was amazing.' They were on and off until 2004 when they permanently reunited. They soon had two children and tied the knot in July 2021 after a decade-long engagement.

The sudden urge to write ballads professing deep, eternal love was understandable given that love stories were unfolding for multiple girls during this time. While Emma was privately building the foundations of her own partnership, another member of the girl group was in a very public whirlwind of her own.

Victoria Adams met Manchester United football prodigy David Beckham in the players' lounge after a match again Chelsea on 22 February 1997, however, their first interaction was brief and inconsequential. The Spice Girls' manager, avid football fan Simon Fuller, enthusiastically pointed David out from across the room to a confused Victoria. 'There he is. David Beckham. You know, the one you said you fancied,' Simon whispered in Victoria's ear. On that day, David and Victoria only exchanged pleasantries and bashful smiles, but it was enough to make a lasting impression on Victoria. Although she hadn't worn her glasses and was a little tipsy from a glass (or two) of champagne, she had enough clarity to note that David was attractive, charming, and that when the other players headed off to the bar, he hung back with his parents and sister, something Victoria found endearing.

Victoria had no idea who David was and couldn't even say with confidence whether he played for Manchester or Chelsea. She didn't understand why Simon was convinced she fancied him but she was finally able to piece the story together when Mel C helped jog her memory. The Spice Girls were cover stars of a December 1996 edition of football magazine *90 Minutes* and for the photoshoot they each donned the kit of a different team. During the post-photoshoot interview, when asked which football player she fancied, Victoria was bored. Football had never interested her in the slightest and as she flipped through the interviewer's flashcards bearing photos of players, she was unimpressed. Finally, she doubled back to one she'd previously overlooked. 'He looks nice. What's his name?' she asked. And that was how David Beckham first appeared on Victoria's radar.

When Simon offered Mel C and Victoria tickets to another Manchester United game a few weeks later they both happily accepted the invitation. She met David for the second time on 15 March 1997 after his match against Sheffield Wednesday and this time Victoria approached him with more confidence. Sparks flew during their first real conversation and the exchange ended with Victoria scribbling her phone number onto the only available piece of paper she had, an airline boarding pass that David still has all these years later.

Their early courtship was shrouded in secrecy. 'Look, you've only just met the guy,' Simon warned according to Victoria's 2001 memoir *Learning To Fly*. 'Before you get photographed, you want to make sure you like each other, because it's a tremendous amount of pressure to put on two people who don't even know each other.' To avoid the gaze of paparazzi, they went on drives together, chatted in shadowy carparks, and occasionally grabbed dinner at hole-in-the-wall establishments in small towns outside of the city. On one evening when they were feeling particularly daring, they went to the cinema, relying on the darkness of the theatre to protect their anonymity. A couple months into this routine, Victoria and David were greeted by gaggle of paparazzi during a meetup in Worsley. News of their romance was out. Victoria suspected that someone had tipped off the press but secretly she was pleased—they would no longer have to sneak around.

With their relationship out in the open, they became a national obsession. A boyish heartthrob heralded as one of the best footballers of all time linking up with a gorgeous world-famous popstar was a match made in heaven. They were stylish, glamourous, and aspirational. Their photos graced newspaper covers on a daily basis and they were quickly nicknamed 'Posh and Becks', a term so ubiquitous around the turn of the millennium that it was added to the *Collins Concise English Dictionary* in 2001. Their public appearances together drew significant attention—every airport trip, every weekend away. Interviews with their cleaning staff made the papers, as did observations by those who happened to briefly stand next to them while shopping. After less than a year of dating, David proposed on 24 January 1998 and they announced their engagement the next day during a press conference in Cheshire. The beaming couple embraced for cameras and Victoria proudly flashed her engagement ring, a 6-carat marquise-cut diamond on a gold band then valued at $85,000.

But Victoria, who had undergone a baptism by fire during the Spice Girls' meteoric rise, knew that not all the attention would be positive and steeled herself for media backlash. Salacious headlines about David's supposed infidelities became a regular occurrence and when his performance on the pitch was anything short of perfection, angry fans blamed Victoria for being a distraction. This intensified after David was thrown out of an England vs Argentina match at the 1998 World Cup for kicking Diego Simeone. Enraged England supporters concluded that David was unfocused and that his personal life was the cause. A wave of vitriol was hurled at David as well as Victoria, who at the time was touring the US with the Spice Girls and had just learned that she was pregnant. At games the crowd regularly chanted, 'Posh Spice takes it up the arse', an embarrassing experience for Victoria, but the hate sometimes veered from cruel into downright terrifying—the couple was targeted by stalkers who mailed bullets to their home. But in times of hardship, they leaned on one another for support. 'Love at first sight does exist,' Victoria wrote in a 2017 letter to her younger self, published in *British Vogue*. 'Even when you don't necessarily want the same thing, your support for each other will mean that you will stick together and grow up together. And it will be worth it.'

In March of 1999, the couple welcomed their first child and four months later, Victoria and David married in an opulent ceremony on the sprawling grounds of Luttrellstown Castle outside of Dublin, Ireland. Victoria wore a custom Vera Wang wedding gown during the ceremony before her and David changed into playfully garish matching purple reception outfits by Antonio Berardi. Guests raised glasses of rose champagne and were waited on by a staggering 437 staff members. With an 18-piece orchestra, a £30,000 tiara perched atop Victoria's head, and literal thrones for the couple to sit in, the wedding was a star-studded spectacle that cost an estimated £750,000. 'As you hold me close so tenderly and watch you fall to sleep / I see in you the one who now completes the half of me I used to be,' Victoria sings during the third verse of 'Time Goes By'. They are the thoughts of a young woman swooning over the newfound love of her life, a love that would stand the test of time.

Not everyone was touched by the unbridled emotion on display in 'Time Goes By'. Alexis Petridis of *The Guardian* bitingly said the track, 'crawls along like a Soviet state funeral'. Mel B chose the song as one of her favourite tracks on *Forever* but seemed to acknowledge its pacing issues even when singing its praises. 'It's very very slow and it can be a bit UGH,' she said, making an exhausted and horrified face. Not exactly a ringing endorsement. 'But if you actually listen to it, when you start off in a good mood and not a depressed mood, it's just so lovely.' Straight from the band's mouth: it's a love song exclusively for those who are blissfully in love.

### 'IF YOU WANNA HAVE SOME FUN'
Duration: 5:26
Written by James Samuel 'Jimmy Jam' Harris III, Terry Lewis, Victoria Beckham, Melanie Brown, Emma Bunton & Melanie Chisholm
Produced and arranged by Jimmy Jam & Terry Lewis
All musical instruments performed by Jimmy Jam & Terry Lewis
Engineered and mixed by Steve Hodge
Assisted by Brad Yost & Xavier Smith
Vocals by Tony Salter

In September 1999, for the first time in their decades-long partnership, prolific R&B songwriting and production team Jimmy Jam and Terry Lewis left their studio in Minneapolis, Minnesota and travelled abroad to London's Whitfield Street studios to collaborate with four young pop sensations. Their credits already included chart-topping singles with prominent performers such as Mariah Carey, Janet and Michael Jackson, Mary J. Blige, Prince, and George Michael but they hadn't strayed from their home base until their writing sessions with the Spice Girls. 'I think it's a great project for us to do because I think it brings a style of songwriting that we don't get a chance to do a lot,' Jimmy said of the opportunity.

Jam and Lewis first met when they were students at Washburn High School in Minneapolis and forged a fast friendship over a shared love of music. This friendship blossomed into a creative partnership and together they wrote, produced, and performed music that blended elements of R&B, jazz, soul and funk, in the process shaping what would be called the Minneapolis sound. In 1981, fellow Minneapolis native Prince assembled a funk band called The Time and due to their stellar reputation, it wasn't long before Jam and Lewis were enlisted to play keyboard and bass, respectively. Even as they toured, they couldn't shake off their first love of producing, something that led to their eventual firing from The Time when they missed a gig because of production work. But being fired presented a new opportunity. They applied what they'd learned from the studio and on the road to their new record label Flyte Tyme Productions Inc., a reference to their first funk band together, Flyte Tyme. Under this label they could freely flex their creative muscles and, in the process, they acquired 22 Grammy nominations and five wins, all of which they collected while clad in their signature looks: black suits, black sunglasses, and black fedoras.

In traditional Spice fashion, the writing session for 'If You Wanna Have Some Fun' was fast and efficient to accommodate busy schedules. 'We're really crunched for time, so we're trying to do two songs in four days, which isn't bad to try and sing that much. But to actually write the songs from scratch...' Jimmy remarked of the tight turnaround, his voice trailing off with worry. He and Terry had come prepared, armed with five rough track ideas from which the band chose two to further develop together. The Spice Girls brainstormed some lyrical and melodic variants and these were incorporated into the finished product. Mere moments after finalizing the lyrics the girls were escorted into the booth to record. 'That's the way we like to work,' Jimmy said during an interview with Kare 11 News. 'It's almost better if you can get it while everybody is still fresh on it and still excited about it, then I think the excitement comes through on the vocals a lot of the time.'

Although buried at the end of the album, 'If You Wanna Have Some Fun' encapsulates the duality of *Forever* when the girls ask, 'Wink wink, nudge nudge / Tell me do you like the rudest stuff?' The band had grown up both professionally and as individuals and the track manages to successfully balance this newfound sense of maturity with the playfulness that was a hallmark on their earlier albums. While other tracks on the album attempt this same tightrope walk with mixed results, the outcome on 'If You Wanna Have Some Fun' is a saucy snapshot of a night out on the prowl for a new flame. In a November 2000 review of *Forever* for *Rolling Stone*, writer James Hunter is reproachful of the album's general forgettability but highlights this track as a bright spot. 'Toward the end of the album [...], Minneapolis geniuses Jimmy Jam and Terry Lewis stroll up and produce "If You Wanna Have Some Fun",' he remarked. 'Fluid and tart, it's one terrific new Spice Girls track, a virtuoso nailing of their milk-and-rhinestones thing lusciously tweaked into champagne and diamonds.'

The song was beloved within the band as well. When asked about her favourite track on the new album, Victoria was quick to answer. 'Mine is "If You Wanna Have Some Fun" because it's got such an old school kind of swing beat, and also because it's been written by Jam and Lewis, who I've always been a big fan of,' she said glowingly. 'I love "If You Wanna Have Some Fun" because it's very old-school and very cheeky,' Emma concurred, also choosing the track as the album's pinnacle. When Geri left the Spice Girls, the band had to learn how to write music for four voices instead of five and Emma's vocals became an integral part of *Forever*'s sound—'If You Wanna Have Some Fun' is one of her shining moments. For the last minute and a half of the track, the thrumming chorus loops with Emma adding vocal flourishes on top. 'Are you having fun?' she asks, the contrast of her bright voice popping over the steady R&B backing. 'I'm hitting notes that I never thought I could've,' Emma squealed with delight about her performance on *Forever* in a July 2000 interview with Edith Bowman for an MTV Making the Video segment. 'I think our vocals are much stronger, the American producers are really pushing the vocal stuff. That's been great and we've learned so much.'

Despite the band, critics, and fans all identifying the song as a perfect Spice Girls single, the track was never released after album sales failed to meet expectations and plans for additional singles were abandoned. Had the swagger and sass of 'If You Wanna Have Some Fun' hit the radio waves public perception of the album could have softened as it possessed many of the qualities detractors felt *Forever* was lacking, most importantly the hallmark Spiciness. 'We didn't want it to sound like Jam and Lewis,' Jimmy said. 'We wanted it to sound like the Spice Girls.'

### 'OXYGEN'
Duration: 4:57
Written by James Samuel 'Jimmy Jam' Harris III, Terry Lewis, Victoria Beckham, Melanie Brown, Emma Bunton & Melanie Chisholm
Produced and arranged by Jimmy Jam & Terry Lewis
All musical instruments performed by Jimmy Jam & Terry Lewis
Engineered and mixed by Steve Hodge
Assisted by Brad Yost & Xavier Smith
Vocals by Tony Salter

'When you listen to this song it kind of takes you to another place,' Emma told *Insider Spice*. The ballad is the second of two songs that the Spice Girls wrote with Jimmy Jam and Terry Lewis during their packed week together in mid-September 1999. Inside London's Whitfield Street studios, the gang slowed their pace after crafting the groovy 'If You Wanna Have Some Fun' and set their sights on fashioning an earnest ballad.

Jam and Lewis instructed the Spice Girls to retreat to separate areas in the studio to quietly reflect on what love meant to them. The resulting meditations were personal and translated effectively into distinct verses about what defines a true partnership—having someone to fight for you when you cannot fight for yourself, living on a foundation of trust that is free of judgement, and nurturing an emotional connection even when separated by distance. The four singers reconvene to deliver the silky-smooth chorus: 'You're the breath that I take / You're the smile on my face / Every time I breathe in / Brings me warmth from within / When you touch me I start believing / Loving is like oxygen.' The track concludes with a soaring key change led by Emma's airy tone. 'It's very uplifting, yet sad at the same time,' Emma said of the song. 'It's just very emotional.'

In a November 2000 edition of *Billboard*, writer Michael Paoletta praised the more mature version of the Spice Girls that was showcased on *Forever* during ballads like 'Oxygen'. '[T]he gals delve deep into love of a far more adult nature—and they do so with more gusto and more soul than ever before,' he wrote. 'Although it takes a moment to get used to the concept of a "serious" Spice Girls, they pull it off quite nicely, often conjuring images of an Anglo-fied Destiny's Child. It's a dicey move for an act whose career is built on frivolity, but it's also a wise one.' Mark Elliott of *uDiscoverMusic* agreed that Jam and Lewis' contributions to the album elevated it at the time of release and have also aged gracefully. 'The Darkchild influence dominates [the album], but it's actually the two Jam and Lewis cuts—"If You Wanna Have Some Fun" and atmospheric slowie "Oxygen"—that have dated better,' he wrote in a 2023 retrospective on the album. 'There's a lightness of touch on those two songs that adds a glance back to a fresher, less mannered time.'

The praise for 'Oxygen' can perhaps be attributed to Jam and Lewis's prowess as producers. In a November 2022 interview with Jay Connor of *The Root*, Jimmy Jam stressed the importance of understanding the psychology of a performer to get the best out of them. He revealed that during the *Forever* sessions, he discovered that Victoria delivered her best vocals when standing under a spotlight. Armed with that knowledge, he made sure that Victoria was bathed in light during her takes. He was committed to doing whatever he could to ensure the artist was comfortable and capable of a strong performance. 'That's the kind of people we like working with,' Mel B said of the Spice Girls' dynamic with Jam & Lewis. 'Really sweet and really down to earth and really just, like, easy going and nice to work with.' The band raved consistently about the duo while promoting *Forever* and the affection was reciprocated, with Jam and Lewis applauding the girl group's focus, comradery, and work ethic. 'I can't think of a more fun experience than working with the Spice Girls,' Jimmy said. 'I thought it was absolutely tremendous.'

8

# *Greatest Hits*

The Spice Girls' *Greatest Hits* was released in the UK on 7 November 2007, where it peaked at No. 2 and was certified double platinum. It sold over 3 million copies worldwide, making it the world's best-selling girl group album of 2007. It featured 13 beloved songs from the band's original run, nine of which were No. 1 hits in the UK, as well as two new tracks recorded that year.

'HEADLINES (FRIENDSHIP NEVER ENDS)'
Duration: 3:30
Written by Spice Girls, Matt Rowe & Richard Stannard
Produced by Matt Rowe & Richard Stannard
Mixed by Mark 'Spike' Stent
Recorded by David Treahearn, Jake Davies, Rob Haggett & Sawas Iosiffidis
Keyboards by Matt Rowe & Richard Stannard
Additional keyboards by David Treahearn & Rob Haggett
Guitar by John Themis & Paul Gendler
Strings performed by Wired Strings
Strings arranged by Rosie Danvers
Released as a single on 5 November 2007

A shadowy, plum-coloured lounge sits empty and silent, a warm glow emitting from a chandelier overhead. The quiet is pierced by the creaking of a door through which five women walk. There is a gravity to their procession as they take their respective places around the lavish space. For the first time since 1998 all five Spice Girls are sharing the same physical space for a music video. As the first plucks of the guitar reverberate, a familiar voice sounds out. 'The time is now or never / To fit the missing piece / To take this on together / You make me feel complete,' Emma sings, her vocals as crisp and light as they were throughout the '90s. The wind machines are in full force as the group begins to croon serenely, styled in sophisticated garments designed by Roberto Cavalli. It feels new yet familiar. Victoria performs in strappy lingerie, her new blonde bob marking the beginning of a new style era for the trendsetter. Mel B's signature coils were smoothed into a long and flowy cut and Mel C, styled in a sharp pantsuit, dominates the middle eight with her reliably robust voice: 'And it feels so good / Every bell's gonna ring / Your love is alive and it's making me sing / I could fly wanna cry / Want the whole world to know / We are together come on baby let's go.' From another pop group, the lyrics could be interpreted as a profession of romantic love but with even a passing familiarity of the act's history, one could deduce that the song's subject matter is friendship. Within the darkened room, amidst the heavy décor and the inky fashions, is a streak of ruby red—Geri, the piece of the puzzle that had once been missing, is back home. The Spice Girls had reunited, and 'Headlines (Friendship Never Ends)' was the single accompanying their triumphant return.

Inter-band conversations about a potential comeback began months before the music video was filmed at London's Pinewood Studios in October 2007. 'Before we'd even got the finalised 'yes' from everyone, we started kind of putting words down [and] it was kind of like a prayer,' Geri remembered. 'You know when you put the footwork in, hoping that it's going to happen.' Despite Geri's enthusiasm there were some reservations from other band members. Emma was pregnant with her first child, a son who would be born in August 2007. This meant she would need to hastily relocate to Los Angeles for rehearsals mere weeks after giving birth with a gruelling tour following soon after. Victoria was working tirelessly to establish her own fashion label, the launch of which would follow in September 2008. And Mel C was hesitant about reforming at all—the idea of slipping back into the role of Sporty Spice after forging her path as a solo artist was anxiety inducing and she feared that the group's chemistry may have diminished during their years apart. She ultimately relented under pressure. 'They basically said if I didn't want to do it then they were going to do it anyway,' she reflected in a story in *The Mirror*. 'I didn't want to be the person who stopped it being the complete five. I was scared that I would be the villain.' On 28 June 2007, all five Spice Girls gathered at London's O2 Arena to hold a press conference announcing their world tour and a *Greatest Hits* album, at which point Mel C was relieved to find that time apart had not affected their group dynamic. 'I was nervous about [whether] we still had that magic and when we did the launch in the summer it was there. I just felt the buzz. That's when I really started to get excited,' she said during an appearance on *This Morning*.

With all five girls now on board they reached out to Matt Rowe and Biff Stannard, their tried-and-true collaborators since the very beginning, to further develop their new single. 'To start with it was a little bit disparate because they were dotted all around the world,' Biff said of the geographical and scheduling difficulties. Matt and Biff worked on the track primarily with Geri and Emma and the other girls contributed lyric suggestions and other feedback via email exchanges. 'All of us together came up with the lyric "headlines",' Biff revealed. 'Initially I think some of the girls said they didn't want it to be about being in the papers, but it's not that, it's about the headlines in your real life rather than your public persona; getting married, having kids.' The chorus of the song features lyrics that pledge renewed devotion to their sisterhood. 'Let's make the headlines loud and true / I wanna tell the world I'm giving it all to you,' they harmonise in a chorus that reads like wedding vows. The song is a smooth pop ballad that fits within their catalogue of music that prioritises friendship above all. 'Just remember friendship never ends,' Geri and Victoria sing in the backing vocals of the chorus, a nod to the single that first put them on the map. The group spent a couple weeks at work in Abbey Road Studios in London before finally recording it at Chalice Studios in Los Angeles. For Biff, it was a meaningful experience. 'They are the easiest act to work with because you know exactly what you have to do. You know straight away who will do what in a song because their personalities are so easy to read. It's great fun and kind of effortless,' he said.

The 'Headlines' music video premiered on 2 November 2007 with the commercial single release following on 19 November. Never one to shy away from brand endorsements, the Spice Girls established a partnership with Victoria's Secret appointing them as the exclusive US retailer of *Greatest Hits* and performed 'Headlines' for the first time at the Victoria's Secret Fashion Show in Los Angeles' Kodak Theater on 16 November 2007. In the United Kingdom, the song was selected as the official single of Children in Need 2007 with all profits donated to the charity appeal. The band quickly learned that the public's affection had survived their hiatus—*Greatest Hits* sold over 3 million copies worldwide and their show at London's O2 Arena sold out in a mere 38 seconds prompting the addition of a staggering 16 additional performances, all of which sold out as well. The other tour stops in England, Canada, the United States, Germany and Spain followed suit. 'How lucky are we to be in a position to be able to do this,' Victoria remarked on the eve of the tour's launch in Vancouver, Canada. 'We're really appreciating every single minute. Before we were so much younger and we were so busy. To get another chance is just fantastic, we're enjoying every second'. Their return was embraced enthusiastically and the incredible success of the reunion was undeniable. The single, however, was their first to stall outside of the Top 10 in the UK where it peaked at No. 11. 'It's really beautiful,' Mel C gushed on Radio 1. 'Anybody who loved the old Spice Girls stuff is going to love this.' The public, however, was divided. While some felt that it captured the spirit of the Spice Girls during their heyday and measured up to ballads like '2 Become 1' and 'Viva Forever', others felt it paled in comparison and lacked their signature spice. Journalists also jumped at the chance to recreate media narratives of the '90s. 'Is it true that Victoria only sings 4 lines on the new single?' Graham Norton asked Mel C during an appearance on his talk show, the audience laughing along knowingly. But Mel C defended her bandmate. 'I think everyone has an equal part in the song,' she emphasised.

'Headlines' is a song about lifelong friendships that emerge on the other side of hardship even stronger. The Return of the Spice Girls Tour provided the girls with concrete proof of their lasting power as both friends and as a band. 'Just to be out there again and look to the left and right of me and see the other girls... that's all I can wish for really,' Emma said, her voice thick with emotion. Fans of the band were likewise moved to see all five girls together again on stage like no time had passed.

## 'Voodoo'
Duration: 3:11
Written by Spice Girls, Matt Rowe & Richard Stannard
Produced by Matt Rowe & Richard Stannard
Mixed by Mark 'Spike' Stent

'Voodoo' is a lively track brimming with funk and attitude in which the Spice Girls urge listeners to, 'Get up and use your voodoo / Get your booty to the floor!' The song was penned by all five Spice Girls in 1998 with help from Matt and Biff but it never made it to the band's third album—Geri departed, Mel B and Victoria got pregnant and went on leave, and then the group decided to explore opportunities with different production teams. It was abandoned before they could record it.

After sitting undeveloped for almost a decade, the song received a second chance at life when the band reunited in 2007. 'I'm really pleased with it,' Biff told *Music Week* in November 2007. 'We just wanted to make an over-the- top, crazy party record like 'Wannabe', with lots of made-up words and nonsense and with everyone enjoying themselves.' The Spice Girls recaptured the infectious fun that was their specialty in the '90s, pulling listeners swiftly into a celebration alongside them. 'Hey, hey, hey, hey, party-la' the quintet sings in unison, a silly ad-lib reminiscent of the infamous 'Zig-a-zig-ah'. While the song doesn't achieve the same level of pop perfection that the Spice Girls were churning out at their peak, 'Voodoo' remains a high-spirited addition to their catalogue that fits in seamlessly. '"Voodoo" goes for the party swing with bumping beats and vocal swagger,' wrote Senior Editor of *IGN*, Spence D. in a November 2007 review of *Greatest Hits*. 'It's typical [Spice Girls] material, drawing heavily upon '80s styled studio funk and electro shock. If not designated as a new track it could easily have been mistaken as a studio outtake from 10 years prior.' Any charm it lacks simply reflects that their reunion was predicated on nostalgia rather than the start of a new era, something that was no secret. 'There's two new tracks on the album, "Voodoo" and "Headlines". That will be it,' Victoria clarified in a November 2007 interview with *Yahoo! Music*. 'This isn't the Spice Girls getting back together to record loads of new material and do a new film. We're not starting off our careers again; we're literally celebrating the past, celebrating our huge success, saying thank you to our fans, showing our kids what we used to do, and finishing it off the way we should have finished it off.'

# 9

# Unreleased Tracks

While these Spice Girls tracks have never been formally released, their existence has been confirmed through live performances, online leaks, or in interviews with the band and their co-writers. Some have surfaced in rough snippets, while others have never been heard but they hint at what remains locked away in the Spice vault. 'There are other demos,' the *Daily Mail* confirmed in a 2021 interview with Biff. 'I'd like the other demo releases to happen too, of course I would. You've got to remember that there's five girls—it's their decision, it's not mine.' The tracks are listed below in alphabetical order.

### 'A Day in Your Life'
A smooth and airy midtempo bop that the Spice Girls wrote with Eliot Kennedy in the summer of 1999. Packed with flamenco guitars, the girls urge listeners to 'dance like there's nobody watching you and you've gotta love like you've never been hurt'. In 2015, a demo recording of the track was released on SoundCloud before promptly being pulled down.

### 'Angels'
'Angels' was first written by Heiðrún Anna Björnsdóttir, a musician best known for her involvement in the Icelandic band Cigarette who found success in the mid-'90s. 'I played my song "Angels" for Simon [Fuller] at this meeting and he was very adamant that it should be the Spice Girls' comeback song,' she told the Icelandic tabloid *DV* in 2019. 'I was just dancing on my way to the bank because he was adamant that it would be a global hit and sell 5 million copies, and then it just didn't

happen—as is often the case in this business.' The track was retooled with input from the Spice Girls as well as writers Luc Emile Leroy and Stephane Mickael Mace Yann. Despite Simon's initial enthusiasm, the track was later jettisoned in favour of 'Headlines'.

### 'C.U. Next Tuesday'
The Spice Girls wrote this liberated breakup song with Matt and Biff during the 1995 *Spice* sessions. '[This one is] a bit rude when you look at the initials of the title,' Biff told author David Sinclair, explaining that it was deemed too risqué to include on their debut album. The full song leaked online in December 2022, after which rumours surfaced that the band was upset that people were listening to the dated track. 'It is obviously a bit embarrassing given the cringeworthy title, as they wouldn't use the c-word in their own lives,' an alleged insider told *The Sun*. In her memoir, Mel C compared the song to Lily Allen's irreverent style that would debut a decade later.

### 'Can't Stay Tonight'
A rousing ballad with a saxophone interlude written with Biff Stannard and Matt Rowe in the summer of 1997. The recorded demo features vocals from only Mel C.

### 'Do You Think About Me'
A slow jam led by Victoria's low timber, 'Do You Think About Me' is one of the band's earliest demos from when the band was still performing under the name Touch. The Spice Girls performed it during an acapella medley on MTV's *Hanging Out* in April 1996. It was written by Alan Glass, Roger Russell, and George Trevorson from Heart Management's stable of writers.

### 'Don't Break My Heart'
Written by Alan Glass and George Robertson MacFarlane circa 1994, the track opens with a dramatic piano intro before shifting into a pop gear. 'It's so plain to see that a love like this was meant to be,' Mel B sings earnestly in the chorus.

### 'Don't You Wanna Be'
'I don't wanna be with nobody else,' the girls sing in the chorus of this Touch-era demo, another simplistic but sweet pop song about new love written by Alan Glass, Roger Russell, and George Trevorson.

## 'Go Go Go'

Recorded with Biff in the summer of 1999, 'Go Go Go' was ultimately left off *Forever* when the album shifted towards a more R&B sound. In 2023, a vinyl record featuring the unreleased song was put up for sale on eBay. While the item was pulled down before the sale was finalised, incomplete vocal, guitar, and drum stems eventually leaked online giving fans a taste of the sassy pop track.

## 'I Want You, I Need You'

A 1994 performance of 'I Want You, I Need You' is featured in ITV's *Raw Spice* documentary. It's a bouncy love song led by Mel C with the other five girls providing a playfully light backing of harmonised sound effects. 'Ba-ba-ba-da ba-ba-ba-da-ee-ya,' they croon while snapping and swaying in unison.

## 'Give You What You Want (If It's Lovin' On Your Mind)'

A quintessentially '90s-sounding track with a punchy beat written with Eliot Kennedy in August 1999. It's classic pop feel pushed it outside of appetite for *Forever* but after leaking online in 2015, fans celebrated its original Spice Girls sound.

## 'Image & Likeness'

An unheard number allegedly written in the *Spiceworld* era. The song has been registered in BMI's licensing database and is credited exclusively to the five Spice Girls.

## 'Is This Really Love'

A Touch-era mid-tempo ballad steered by Mel C's powerful vocals. The song is credited to writers Alan Glass, Elizabeth Martin, and Bizi in the BMI licensing database.

## 'Just One of Those Days'

An unheard track from the band's tenure as Touch, the first written with input from all five Spice Girls with help from writers Chris Arms and Alan Glass. 'We sat around the table in the dining room one night and started humming a melody,' Geri recalled in her memoir *If Only*. 'I chipped in with a line that fitted and then someone else added another.' It was a turning point for the group who realised that if they were dissatisfied with the material at their disposal, they could simply write their own.

### 'Leader of The Gang'
The Spice Girls covered this Gary Glitter track, originally written with Mike Leander, for a performance scene in *Spice World The Movie* but the studio recording was dropped from the *Spiceworld* album and Gary Glitter's appearance was cut from the film after he was arrested for possession of child pornography.

### 'Melody of Life'
Written in the 1995 *Spice* sessions, snippets of 'Melody of Life' leaked online revealing the track to be a groovy R&B pop number.

### 'Overnight'
A track from the band's 1995 *Spice* sessions that Mel C referenced in her memoir, revealing it, 'was about a sex worker doing what she had to do to survive'. It was salvaged from the cutting room floor in 1999 and another demo was recorded with help from Matt and Biff but it was abandoned a second time and omitted from *Forever*. Neither the 1995 nor the 1999 demo has surfaced to date.

### 'Pain Proof'
In the summer of 1999, the Spice Girls wrote 'Pain Proof' with Eliot Kennedy, a funky pop-rock track about the band's resilience in the face of an invasive tabloid media. 'We're pain proof and nothing you can do can touch us,' they taunt.

### 'Perfect Vision'
A small snippet of this Touch-era demo leaked online showing only the first seeds of a potential track. The five girls can be heard harmonising the song's only lyrics: 'Perfect Vision'.

### 'Pleasin' Me'
A track that all five girls wrote with Matt and Biff for *Spice*—it was registered with the music rights management company BMI but has never been shared publicly.

### 'Power of 5'
The Spice Girls wrote 'Power of 5' with Biff for their Channel 5 launch campaign. 'Take it from us, it's Girl Power! Take it from us, it's the Power of 5,' they cry in the lively track that was featured in a colourful television ad featuring the band. The song nods to Manfred Mann's 1964 song '5-4-3-2-1'.

### 'Serial Killer'
While demos have never surfaced publicly this *Spice*-era track was confirmed to exist by Mel C in her 2022 memoir.

### 'Seven Days'
Written with Mark Taylor and Sheppard Solomon who went on to have booming songwriting careers. Mark worked closely with artists including Cher, Tina Turner, Whitney Houston, and Kylie Minogue while Sheppard proceeded to write with Celine Dion, Britney Spears, Kelly Clarkson, and One Direction. Sheppard didn't find the Spice Girls' concentrated pop sound compelling and while the band expressed interest in continued collaboration, he declined. 'That was one of the biggest mistakes I made,' he revealed during an interview on podcast *Iconography: The Original Doll with James Rodriguez*.

### 'Sound Off / Military Cadence'
For *Spice World The Movie*, the band recorded their own spiced up version of the call-and-response singalong popularised by the United States Military. 'We're the Spice Girls, yes indeed / Just girl power is all we need.'

### 'Spice Is Back'
The Spice Girls wrote 'Spice Is Back' around the time of the band's 2007 reunion and subsequently registered the track with BMI for licensing purposes. The five girls cowrote it with Greg Hatwell, the long-time guitarist in Mel C's touring band for her solo work.

### 'Strong Enough'
A rough demo of this funky synth track, believed to originate from the 1995 *Spice* sessions with Eliot Kennedy, leaked online, revealing some of the band's early female empowerment messaging with a chorus asking, 'Are you strong enough to control your life?'

### 'Sugar & Spice'
This slinky track inspired the band to change their name from Touch to Spice. Despite its impact on their long-term branding, the song was never released, however, a partial demo later leaked online. It was written circa 1994 with Tim Hawes, a songwriter and producer who went on to find success writing material for acts like Aaron Carter and Sugababes.

### 'Take Me Away'

A sultry number from their days as Touch written by Erwin Keiles and John Thirkell, members of the musical production team with Heart Management. A performance of this song circa 1994 appeared in the documentary *Raw Spice* released by *ITV* in 2001 and was later recorded by Heart Management's The Three Degrees, a Philadelphia soul trio.

### 'Too Hot'

Recorded with Biff in the summer of 1999, the track was ultimately left off *Forever* when the album shifted towards an R&B sound. In 2023, a vinyl record featuring the unreleased song was put up for sale on eBay. The item was pulled down before the sale was finalised but snippets of the girls purring 'Hot like fire' leaked online.

### 'W.O.M.A.N.'

This disco-inspired romp was performed live by the band on the 1999 Christmas in Spiceworld Tour but was omitted from their third album released the next year. The band's decision to shelve the song was disappointing to Biff, who felt it perfectly set up the band's next era. 'I thought that song was really interesting lyrically, because it was making the progression from girls to women, which was something I thought it was time for them to do,' he told author David Sinclair. 'They needed something to suggest that they were still the same group of friends, but they were gaining more maturity.'

### 'Walking On Air'

This retro-sounding R&B track was one of the band's earliest demos from their era as Touch and was written by Alan Glass, Roger Russell, and George Trevorson.

### 'We're Gonna Make It Happen'

A song from their days as Touch, the band tirelessly rehearsed harmonies and dance routines to this upbeat and snappy pop track that stated their intention to find success as a group. Performance footage of this song filmed in 1994 appeared in the 2001 ITV documentary *Raw Spice*. In a behind-the-scenes video from the 2019 Spice World Tour, Geri, Mel B, Mel C and Emma jokingly sang the chorus to warm up before a show. 'The first song we ever did,' Geri exclaimed with laughter at the full-circle moment.

# Bibliography

## MUSIC

Spice Girls, *Spice*—Published by Windswept Pacific Music Ltd., PolyGram Music Publishing Ltd., Sony/ATV Music Publishing, Chrysalis Music Ltd., 19 Music, and BMG Music Publishing. Copyright Virgin Records Ltd. Recorded at Olympic Studios & Strongroom. 1996.

Spice Girls, *Spiceworld*—Published by 19 Music, BMG Music Publishing Ltd., Copyright Control, PolyGram Music Publishing Ltd., and Windswept Pacific Music Ltd. Copyright Virgin Records Ltd. Recorded at Abbey Road Studios, Lansdowne Studios, Manor Mobile, Olympic Studios, and Whitfield Street Studios. 1997.

Spice Girls, *Forever*—Published by Published by EMI Music Publishing Ltd., Sony/ATV Harmony UK, PeerMusic (UK) Ltd., BMG Rights Management (UK) Ltd., Universal Music Publishing MGB Ltd., Nights Time Songs Ltd., SM Music Publishing Ltd., EMI Music Publishing (WP) Ltd., Universal Music Publishing. Copyright Virgin Records Ltd. 2000.

## BOOKS

Beckham, V., *Learning To Fly* (London: Penguin Group 2001)
Bravo, L., *What Would The Spice Girls Do?* (London: Bantam Press 2018)
Brown, M., *Catch A Fire* (London: Headline Book Publishing 2002)
Chisholm, M., *The Sporty One* (New York: Grand Central Publishing 2022)
Doctor Spice, *The Doctor Spice Collection* (North Haven: Kindle Direct Publishing 2022)
Halliwell, G., *If Only* (London: Bantam Books 1999)

Jackson, J. A., *A House On Fire: The Rise and Fall of Philadelphia Soul* (New York: Oxford University Press 2004)

Sinclair, D., *Wannabe: How The Spice Girls Reinvented Pop* (London: Omnibus Press 2004)

Smith, S., *Spice Girls: The Story of the World's Greatest Girl Band* (London: HarperCollins Publishers 2019)

The Spice Girls, *Forever Spice* (London: Little, Brown and Company 1999)

The Spice Girls, *Girl Power!* (London: Zone/Chameleon Books 1997)

The Spice Girls, *Real Life: Real Spice: The Official Story* (London: Zone/VCI Books 1997)

The Spice Girls, *Spiceworld: The Official Book of The Movie* (London: Ebury Press 1997)

## ARTICLES

'4 Spice Girls Tried To Seduce Me; My three-year love affair with Baby Emma' (*The Free Library*, www.thefreelibrary.com 1997). Accessed 10 April 2024.

'A Spice day for a white wedding; Tearful Mel B is Mrs G' (*The Free Library*, www.thefreelibrary.com 1998). Accessed 10 April 2024.

Barrett, C., 'Spice Girls: The Singers' Songwriters' (*Music Week*, www.proquest.com 2007). Accessed 10 April 2024.

Beckham, V. 'Dear Victoria: Mrs Beckham Pens A Letter To Her 18-Year-Old Self' (*British Vogue*, www.vogue.co.uk 217). Accessed 10 April 2024.

Bird, D., 'Mel B Was "In the Middle" as She Represented Mixed-Race Women in Spice Girls' (*Mirror*, www.mirror.co.uk 2023). Accessed 10 April 2024.

Boyle, S., 'Spice Girls mortified by re-emergence of X-rated demo of song with filthy title' (*The Sun*, www.thesun.co.uk 2022). Accessed 10 April 2024.

Brown, M. '"We Knew We Were Different" Mel B reveals how her dad had to carry her around as a baby to avoid being attacked by racists' (*The Sun*, www.thesun.co.uk 2021). Accessed 10 April 2024.

Browne, D., 'Music Review: Spiceworld' (*Entertainment Weekly*, www.ew.com 1997). Accessed 10 April 2024.

Browne, D., 'Music Review: Forever' (*Entertainment Weekly*, www.ew.com 2000). Accessed 10 April 2024.

Bruton, L., 'The Spice Girls In Stoneybatter' (*IMAGE*, www.image.ie 2019). Accessed 10 April 2024.

Bryson, J., 'The Influence of Black Music: How "Flyte Tyme" Changed the World From A Recording Studio' (*North Star Journey*, www.mprnews.org 2023). Accessed 10 April 2024.

Cartner-Morley, J., 'Victoria Beckham: I guess it was a sign of insecurity, wearing very tight clothes' (*The Guardian*, www.theguardian.com 2020). Accessed 10 April 2024.

*Cathy Dennis*, www.cathydennisofficial.com. Accessed 10 April 2024.

Clinton, L.M., 'What the Lyrics to Spice Girls' "Wannabe" Actually Mean' (*Glamour*, www.glamour.com 2015). Accessed 10 April 2024.

Connor, J., '"When You Write Music History, You Can't Leave Us Out": Jimmy Jam and Terry Lewis Stake Their Claim as Music Royalty' (*The Root*, www.theroot.com 2022). Accessed 10 April 2024.

Cooper, G., 'Bookies Lose On Spice Christmas' (*Independent*, www.independent.co.uk 1998). Accessed 10 April 2024.

Cragg, M., 'Emma Bunton: "We made Victoria clean the bathroom!"' (*The Guardian*, www.theguardian.com 2019). Accessed 10 April 2024.

D. S., 'Spice Girls: Greatest Hits Review' (*IGN*, www.ign.com 2012). Accessed 10 April 2024.

Dalton, S., 'What's The Piquancy…?' (*Vox*, www.rocksbackpages.com 1996). Accessed 10 April 2024.

Desborough, J. and Patterson, E., 'The Spice Girls Shoot That Kicked Off "Girl Power" and the S&M Secret That Nearly Scuppered It All' (*Mirror*, www.mirror.co.uk 2016). Accessed 10 April 2024.

Duncan, C., 'Spice Girls' Melanie C Opens Up About Sexuality Speculation' (*Pink News*, www.thepinknews.com 2022). Accessed 10 April 2024.

Elliott, M., 'Forever: Spice Girls' Final Album Brought A Barrage of Brilliant Memories' (*uDiscoverMusic*, www.udiscovermusic.com 2023). Accessed 10 April 2024.

Elterich, G., 'Let's Talk About Sex and Hip Hop: How 90s Rap Helped Stem the AIDS Epidemic' (*Spoven Weedle Presents*, www.spovenweedlepresents.blogspot.com 2018). Accessed 10 April 2024.

'Emma Bunton opens up about reality of filming iconic 2 Become 1 video in "New York"' (*Heart*, https://www.heart.co.uk 2021). Accessed 10 April 2024.

Ferlita, G., 'Spice Girls' Songwriter Claims There Are More Unreleased Tracks in the Archives' (*Daily Mail*, www.dailymail.co.uk 2021). Accessed 10 April 2024.

Garcia, G., 'Close Encounters' (*Phoenix New Times*, www.phoenixnewtimes.com 1998). Accessed 10 April 2024.

Garner, G., 'Hitmakers: The Songwriting Secrets Behind Wannabe' (*MusicWeek*, www.musicweek.com 2020). Accessed 10 April 2024.

Garvin, P., 'Christmas Wrapping: Cover Songs Uncovered' (*Pop Culture Experiment*, www.popcultureexperiment.com 2016). Accessed 10 April 2024.

'Girl power triumphs for second Christmas' (*BBC News*, www.bbc.com/news 1997). Accessed 10 April 2024.

Gordon, J. and Liepins, L., 'Songwriter, Producer Enjoys International Success' (*Richmond Sentinel*, www.richmondsentinel.ca 2023). Accessed 10 April 2024.

Gunnarsdóttir, L. K., 'Heiðrún Samdi Lag Fyrir Spice Girls' (*DV*, www.dv.is 2019). Accessed 10 April 2024. Gupta, A.H. & Harlan, J., 'How the Spice Girls' Manufactured Girl Power Became Real' (*The New York Times*, www.nytimes.com 2022. Accessed 10 April 2024.

Hampp, A., 'Mary Frisbie Wood: Pepsi's Pop Songwriter' (*Billboard*, www.billboard.com 2012). Accessed 10 April 2024.

Hansford, A., 'Melanie C says Spice Girls stood for "Gay Power," not just "Girl Power" (*Pink News*, www.thepinknews.com 2011). Accessed 10 April 2024.

Heath, C., 'Spice Girls: Too Hot To Handle' (*Rolling Stone*, www.rollingstone.com 1997). Accessed 10 April 2024.

Heawood, S., 'Former Spice Girl Geri: "I Like Myself A Bit Better Now"' (*The Guardian*, www.theguardian.com 2016). Accessed 10 April 2024.

Humberstone, N., 'Eliot Kennedy: Producing Sheffield Music' (*Sound On Sound*, www.soundonsound.com 1997). Accessed 10 April 2024.

Hunter, J., 'Forever' (*Rolling Stone*, www.rollingstone.com 2000). Accessed 10 April 2024.

*Insider Spice Magazine*, Issue 10 (*Insider Spice* 2000)

Kale, S., 'How the 'Spice World' Movie Became a Deranged, Postmodern Masterpiece' (*Vice*, www.vice.com 2018). Accessed 10 April 2024.

Kamp, D., 'London Swings! Again!' (*Vanity Fair*, www.vanityfair.com 2007). Accessed 10 April 2024.

Kaplan, I., 'Spice Girls' Spiceworld Turns 20: Remembering Their Eclectic, Theatrical Second Album' (*Billboard*, www.billboard.com 2017). Accessed 10 April 2024.

Lavin, W., 'Spice Girls Have Changed '2 Become 1' Lyrics To Be More LGBTQI-Friendly' (*NME*, www.nme.com 2019). Accessed 10 April 2024.

Lewis, A., 'How the Spice Girls really got their nicknames' (*Stylist*, www.stylist.co.uk 2015). Accessed 10 April 2024.

Lott-Lavigna, R., 'The Untold Story of the Lynchian Video of the Spice Girls' Viva Forever' (*Crack*, www.crackmagazine.net 2017). Accessed 10 April 2024.

McCaffrey, J., 'Catfights, feuds and fall-outs behind the scenes with the Spice Girls' (*The Mirror*, www.mirror.co.uk 2019). Accessed 10 April 2024.

McCarthy, A., 'Spice Girls, Sexualisation and Pre Teen Girls' (*The Irish Times*, www.irishtimes.com 1997). Accessed 10 April 2024.

'McCulloch And Marr Song Beat Out Other Brits for U.K. World Cup Theme' (*MTV*, www.mtv.com 1998). Accessed 10 April 2024.

McGuinness, R. 'Dad cashes in '90s Pepsi ring pulls to claim free Spice Girls CD 26 years later' (*Yahoo News*, uk.news.yahoo.com 2024). Accessed 10 April 2024.

McManus, S. 'It's Been 20 Years Since the Spice Girls' Iconic 1997 BRIT Awards Performance' (*Attitude Magazine*, www.attitude.co.uk 2017). Accessed 23 April 2024.

'Melanie Chisholm Visits Oulton Park Race Track for the First Public Outing of her Brother's OK! Sponsored Sports Car' (*OK! Magazine*, Issue 2 April 1999)

O'Shea, K., 'Did You Know This Spice Girls Music Video Was Filmed In Ireland?' (*IrishCentral*, www.irishcentral.com 2023). Accessed 10 April 2024.

*Official Charts - Home of the Official UK Top 40 Charts*, www.officialcharts.com. Accessed 10 April 2024.

Pacheco, P., 'Aida, Meet Elton' (*Los Angeles Times*, www.latimes.com 1999). Accessed 10 April 2024.

Petridis, A., 'All 43 Spice Girls Songs—Ranked!' (*The Guardian*, www.theguardian.com 2018). Accessed 10 April 2024.

Plotz, D., 'Cherish These Cheeky Hucksters Before They're Gone' (*Slate*, www.slate.com 1997). Accessed 10 April 2024.

Price, M. J., "Christmas Wrapping,' An Unlikely Hit For The Waitresses, Spreads Cheer 40 Years Later' (*Akron Beacon Journal*, www.beaconjournal.com 2021). Accessed 10 April 2024.

Qassim, A., 'How the Band Led the Brand to Expand Pepsi's Marketshare' (*Campaign*, www.campaignlive.co.uk 1997). Accessed 10 April 2024.

Ramesbottom, L., 'Mel B Opens Up About the Racism She Faced At the Height of Spice Girls Fame' (*eTalk*, www.etalk.ca 2020). Accessed 10 April 2024.

'RETRO CHART 1998: "Viva Forever" was the Spice Girls' first No. 1 without Geri Halliwell' (*Irish Independent*, www.independent.ie 2022). Accessed 10 April 2024.

Rigby, S., 'Why Spice Girls' Wannabe is the Catchiest Song of All Time' (*BBC*, www.bbc.com 2016) Accessed 10 April 2024.

Robpop, 'Pop Music! Something To Believe In!' (*Don't Stop The Pop*, www.dontstopthepop.blogspot.com 2008). Accessed 10 April 2024.

Robpop, 'The Richard Stannard Interview' (*Don't Stop The Pop*, www.dontstopthepop.blogspot.com 2008). Accessed 10 April 2024.

Robledo, J., 'Victoria Beckham Shares Heartwarming Encounters With LGBTQ+ Spice Girls Fans' (*GAY TIMES*, www.gaytimes.co.uk 2022). Accessed 10 April 2024.

Seymour, C. 'Spice Girls: Holler Review' (*R&Being*, www.randbeing.com 2000). Accessed 10 April 2024.

'Scary Spice Explains Meaning of "Goodbye" Single' (*MTV*, www.mtv.com 1998). Accessed 10 April 2024.

'Scary Spice Splits with Husband' (*BBC News*, www.bbc.com/news 2000). Accessed 10 April 2024.

Solomon, K., 'How the UK Christmas No 1 Became A National Obsession—and a Vicious Competition' (*The Guardian*, www.theguardian.com 2022). Accessed 10 April 2024.

*Songview; A Combined View of ASCAP and BMI Musical Works*, www.repertoire.bmi.com. Accessed 10 April 2024.

*Spice Girls*, www.thespicegirls.com. Accessed 10 April 2024.

'Spice Girls a sensation in Dublin' (Belfast Telegraph, www.belfasttelegraph.co.uk 1998). Accessed 10 April 2024.

'Spice Girls Backlash Hits the Internet' (*MTV*, www.mtv.com 1997). Accessed 10 April 2024.

'Spice Girls head for top' (*BBC News*, www.bbc.com/news 2000). Accessed 10 April 2024.

'Spice Girls Management Change Sets Tabloids Buzzing' (*MTV*, www.mtv.com 1997). Accessed 10 April 2024.

'Spice Girls Producer Jerkins Promises Urban Feel on New Album' (*MTV*, www.mtv.com 1999). Accessed 10 April 2024.

SpiceGirlsNet, 'Absolute Producer, Paul Wilson on the making of Naked' (www.facebook.com/SpiceGirlsNet Aug 10 2018). Accessed 10 April 2024.

Sullivan, C., 'Oriental Spice - Sponsor Power, Not Bazaars, Draws the Girls to Turkey' (*The Guardian*, www.theguardian.com 1997). Accessed 10 April 2024.

'True Amazing Lives: Baby Spice, by Mummy Spice; Emma Bunton and Her Mother Talk About Their Amazing Bond in the Most Touching Interview Ever' (*The Free Library*, www.thefreelibrary.com 2001). Accessed 10 April 2024.

Victoria and Albert Museum, 'The Making of an Iconic Image: Christine Keeler, 1963' (*V&A*, www.vam.ac.uk 2020). Accessed 10 April 2024.

Vincent, A., 'How Geri Halliwell Created Her Era-Defining Brit Awards Dress' (*The Telegraph*, www.telegraph.co.uk 2017). Accessed 10 April 2024.

Watts, L., 'Richard 'Biff' Stannard, the Man With the X Factor' (*Pink News*, www.thepinknews.com 2011). Accessed 10 April 2024.

'We Fell into the Bunk Bed... Vowing to Stay Together; My 3-Year Love Affair With Baby' (*The Free Library*, www.thefreelibrary.com 2001). Accessed 10 April 2024.

'Wedded spice' (*BBC News*, www.bbc.com/news 1999). Accessed 10 April 2024.

West, D., 'Spice single cash to go to charity' (Digital Spy, www.digitalspy.com 2007). Accessed 10 April 2024.

Wild, D., 'Spiceworld' (*Rolling Stone*, www.rollingstone.com 1997). Accessed 10 April 2024.

Wilson, E., 'Emma Bunton Says Her Split From Husband Jade Jones Gave Them Time to 'Grow as People' (*Mirror*, www.mirror.co.uk 2022). Accessed 10 April 2024.

Yarrow, A., 'How The 90s Tricked Women Into Thinking They'd Gained Gender Equality' (*Time*, www.time.com 2018). Accessed 10 April 2024.

Young, M., 'How the Spice Girls Escaped Their Manager Chris Herbert and Set Upon Their Own Path to Fame' (www.news.com.au 2017). Accessed 10 April 2024.

## Documentaries and Videos

Barnard, D., *Girl Power! Live In Istanbul. Girls Talk! The Story So Far...* (A Fuji International Production / Virgin Records 1997)

Chisholm, M., 'Ask Melanie C Live with Special Guest Biff' (www.youtube.com/@MelanieC 23 April 2020)

Davies, N., *Raw Spice: The Unofficial Story of the Making of the Spice Girls* (ITV 2001)*Kare 11 News Extra,* 'Spice Girls In the Studio with Jimmy Jam and Terry Lewis' (Kare 11 News 1999)

MTV, *Spice Girls – Making the Video; Holler & Let Love Lead the Way* (MTV 2000)

*MuchMusic*. 'Geri Halliwell' (Original Airdate 10 April 1999)

Smeaton, B., *Spice Girls: Giving You Everything* (BBC 2007)

Stratton, S., 'Spice Girls Interview – Forever' (Inflight Studios / Virgin Records 2000)

Vogue, 'Ginger Spice Tells the Story Behind Her Union Jack Dress' (www.youtube.com/@Vogue, 19 March 2020)

Wander, S., *The Spice Girls Story: Viva Forever!* (Burning Bright Productions Limited 2012)

## Podcasts and Radio

*90s Noise*, 'Just Give Me A Good Song Title with Howard Greenhalgh' (Acast, 10 May 2023)

*90s Noise*, '2 Become 1 with Andy Delaney' (Acast, 28 June 2023)

*Desert Island Discs*, 'Melanie C' (BBC Radio 4, 23 February 2020)

McCullough, D., *Gaydio Breakfast*, 'Melanie C Talks To Emma and Dean' (Gaydio, 30 April 2020)

*Music Business Worldwide*, 'Biff Stannard, Songwriter: Spice Girls, Kylie and a Near-Death Experience' (Voly Entertainment, 17 November 2020)

Rodriguez, J., *Iconography: The Original Doll,* 'Don't Stop Movin'' (www.theoriginaldoll.com, 8 April 2024)